LIBERATING
VISIONS

HUMAN FULFILLMENT AND SOCIAL JUSTICE IN AFRICAN-AMERICAN THOUGHT

Robert Michael Franklin

Fortress Press
Minneapolis

LIBERATING VISIONS
Human Fulfillment and Social Justice in
African-American Thought

Cover design: Jim Gerhard.

Cover photos: (clockwise) Martin Luther King, Jr., Religious News Service;
W. E. B. Du Bois, Frederic Lewis, Inc.; Malcolm X, Religious News Service; Booker
T. Washington, Religious News Service.

Library of Congress Cataloging-in-Publication Data

Franklin, Robert Michael, 1954–
    Liberating visions : human fulfillment and social justice in
African-American thought / Robert Michael Franklin.
        p.   cm.
    Includes bibliographical references.
    ISBN 0-8006-2392-4
        1. Afro-Americans—Psychology.   2. Self-realization.   3. Social
justice.   4. Social ethics.   5. Washington, Booker T., 1856–1915.
    6. DuBois, W. E. B. (William Edward Burghardt), 1868–1963.   7. X,
    Malcolm, 1925–1965.   8. King, Martin Luther, Jr., 1929–1968.
I. Title.
E185.F8265   1990
303.3'72'08996073—dc20   89-35979
                                                                              CIP

The paper used in this publication meets the minimum requirements of American
National Standard for Information Sciences—Permanence of Paper for Printed
Library Materials, ANSI Z329.48-1984.   ∞™

Manufactured in the U.S.A.   AF 1-2392
94   93   92   3   4   5   6   7   8   9   10

to my grandmother, Martha McCann
my first and finest moral teacher

✢ Contents ✢

+ PREFACE +

During the cultural revolutions of the 1960s, I came of age. As a junior at Morgan Park High School in Chicago, I discovered the exhilaration that comes from political activism. Watching and listening to people like Dr. Martin Luther King, Jr., the Rev. Jesse Jackson, State Senator Julian Bond, and Congresswoman Barbara Jordan, I learned a good deal about the politics of protest and negotiation. Like so many other student leaders of the time, I observed institutions throughout American society undergo rapid change in response to the vigorous demands of protesting youth. For a fleeting moment in history, buoyed by our scattered successes, many of us felt that we could change the world.

Amid the excitement of the period, however, I often felt uncertain and uneasy about the proper future course. Much was at stake in finding answers to questions concerning the role of violence, Christian faith, women, the church, interracial coalitions, and our own parents in the struggle. Heated arguments broke out between persuasive, charismatic leaders. Confusion among the masses often ensued.

After the death of Dr. King, my father, Robert Franklin, Sr., and I attended numerous rallies and listened to many speeches concerning these matters. Although he was a patient man seeking to nurture my developing political consciousness, he often found to be dubious the claims made by Black Panther Party spokesmen and other young revolutionary leaders concerning the moral necessity of the immediate, cataclysmic demolition of American society. At that time, I could only attribute his response to age rather than advanced wisdom and experience. Nevertheless, his hesitations induced some skepticism within me. At times I found myself wishing that some of the great and proven thinkers and activists of black history could be exhumed so that I could hear their voices on the significant questions facing African Americans and the wider society. This book grows out of my wish to hear again the wisdom of the brilliant and skillful black leaders of the twentieth century. Although the project was formulated during my doctoral studies at the University of Chicago Divinity School, the generative idea emerged years ago in the mind of a teenager who often fantasized hosting a private dinner party for the four figures of this book.

Conversation is the highest form of human activity. I wish that I were better at it. I am indebted to the many high quality conversation partners who have helped to produce this book. I am especially grateful to C. Shelby Rooks (former president of Chicago Theological Seminary), Don Browning, Robin Lovin, and Martin Marty (my dissertation committee) for their patience, encouragement and high expectations.

As noted earlier, the generative idea for this book emerged during my adolescent years, so I must thank those with whom the conversation began. I am indebted to high school dialogue partners Mae Jemison, a classmate who demanded more clarity of thought than any of my teachers. She has since become NASA's first black female astronaut. I am also indebted to vice-principal Dr. William O'Bannon, my most acerbic critic who during my times of rebellion urged upon me Somerset Maugham's, *The Razor's Edge*, the reading of which became a turning point in my life. I am grateful to the faculty of Morehouse College, especially my political science professor Robert Brisbane and college president Hugh Gloster, who were uniformly dedicated to instilling liberating visions in the minds of future leaders. During my graduate studies, a long list of people encouraged and challenged me in my writing and thinking never to separate passion from precision. Many of them read drafts of my work and offered critical comments from which I have learned much. Among them were James Cone, Cornel West, James Evans, Jr.,

Toinette Eugene, Herbert Aptheker, Bennie Goodwin, Vincent Harding, Preston Williams, Peter Paris, Donna Franklin, Samuel and Sheila Hogan, Dorothy and William Cross, and my indexer Joy Browne.

I save the final word of appreciation for those who taught me to take my first steps in life. My pastor, Bishop Louis Ford, was my first model of civil rights activism. He has given more than I can ever return. During my doctoral work, he permitted me to "practice" teaching upon the patient and kind people of St. Paul Church of God in Christ in Chicago. They affectionately call me "Bobby."

I am blessed to have had parents, Robert and Lee Ethel Franklin, who made enormous sacrifices in order to educate me. Their love and support, together with that of my brothers David, Andrew, and Brian, and my sisters Cheryl and Martha Patrice, have sustained me through times of discouragement. I offer thanks to my extended family, the Franklins, McCanns, Battles, and Goffneys, who have each nurtured me in distinctive ways.

Finally, I am thankful for my steadfast companion, Cheryl Goffney Franklin, without whose support and gentle criticism I could not have completed this work.

Introduction

The four men spotlighted in this book, together with other black religious and political leaders and communities, have developed distinctive and significant traditions of moral thinking and social criticism. Their perspective is essential to a genuine intellectual and social history of the United States. The former slaves and their descendants' experience in America stood in sharp contrast to that of the Anglos and European immigrants, and their style of moral thinking possessed the distinctive power and prophetic edge of people who had been, to use Malcolm X's searing phrase, "the victims of democracy." Indeed, they were victims of economic privation, political exclusion, cultural suppression, and systematic psychological and social domination due to the hue of their skin. In defiance of this victimization, amazingly, most of them understood blacks to be American citizens and consistently appropriated and appealed to America's religious and political heritage as, in part, their own. Both the Bible and America's constitutive documents have furnished black moral thinkers with symbols, normative concepts and historical understandings and narratives with which to elaborate the African-American quest for justice and human fulfillment.

Although the principal concern of these thinkers was social justice entailing significant institutional transformations in American society, they were also attentive to the substantive content and formal character of the authentically free life and moral person.

1

Indeed, most of them realized that authentic liberation required personal as well as social transformation.

Historically, many of these thinkers were Christian ministers whose faith commitments informed their visions of the moral person and just society (e.g., Bishop Henry McNeal Turner, the Rev. Henry Highland Garnet, the Rev. Jarena Lee, Bishop Richard Allen). Other leaders were usually Christian laypersons (Frederick Douglass, Booker T. Washington, Sojourner Truth, Harriet Tubman), although some were not explicitly Christian and operated from secular bases of authority in the community (Du Bois). Together, their thoughts on morality, social justice, personal fulfillment, and God have yielded a rich tradition of moral, political, and theological reflection from a black perspective.

Contemporary black theology represents one expression of this broader tradition of moral and political thought. Despite the significance and diversity of perspective in black theology, however, much of it does not adequately attend to the host of issues related to personal identity, wholeness, and fulfillment. This critique is not peculiar to black theology, as it shares with a host of other theological systems a romantic optimism concerning human capacities to transform the social order (Marxist-informed liberation theologies, liberal theologies, and earlier Social Gospel traditions). Once the kingdom of God is achieved, many authors imply, liberated people who are free from the vices of the old order (avarice, sexism, racism, classism, etc.) will emerge as well.

I maintain that these traditions have paid insufficient attention to the manner in which people ought to be transformed and equipped to live in the new society that is thought to be emerging. This general inattention to the personal dimension of the liberation enterprise has important consequences. Failure to understand the person-centered dimension of a broader, inclusive societal transformation can lead to a disturbing paradox: an optimism concerning the future of society existing alongside personal and familial disintegration, despair and frustration. As Parker Palmer insightfully observed in *The Company of Strangers: Christians and the Renewal of America's Public Life*, public and private life somehow needs to be kept in dynamic balance. The most public of persons need the renewing experience of private life to survive because in our private lives we

come to discover and experience intimacy, trust, and the uncon-
ditional acceptance that public life seldom provides. During the
sixties many activists burned out in their public roles, in part because
they had failed to practice a "private rhythm of renewal."[1]

If the humanizing effects of black theology are to be imple-
mented within local parishes and communities, theologians must
focus on the person and the family. They must bring religious resources to bear on the ways people can and should be renewed in
order to become authentically free. (Authentic freedom refers to the
absence of structural and psychological obstacles to achieving personal development, and to the positive capacity to actualize one's
fullest human potential.) Once this has been accomplished, we
should be able to receive a conceptually clear response to the questions, What is the nature of the authentically free life? In the context
of this particular society and culture, who is the good person? Which
virtues, identities, capacities, and commitments are necessary or
sufficient for a life of integrity and fulfillment?

One method for initiating meaningful responses to such questions and for correcting the perspectival imbalance in black theology
is to identify the finest and most-trusted resources and reflections
on personal wholeness in the modern black community and to present them for revision, reconsideration, and possible reappropria-
tion. The time has come for a hermeneutics of recovery.

In this book, I examine visions of human fulfillment and of the
just society as presented by Booker T. Washington (1856–1915),
W. E. B. Du Bois (1868–1963), Malcolm X (1925–1965), and Martin
Luther King, Jr. (1929–1968). Given the vast number of brilliant
and influential African American leaders, my selection of these four
may seem arbitrary. As I examined the ranks of post-Reconstruction
African American leaders, I did so with an eye for those whose
intellectual and political influence upon past and present Americans
could be characterized as *monumental*. I asked, Who possessed a
significant local and international reputation as an effective spokes-
person for oppressed people? Who established institutions or organizations dedicated to the ongoing implementation of their social
visions? Whose ideas would still merit serious reconsideration in
one hundred years?

With these questions in mind, I focused upon leaders who left
a significant corpus of writings and speeches available for analysis.

ach spoke and wrote a considerable amount about in-
plans, community development, social justice, and the
elationships among the three. In his own way, each of
mental public moralists analyzed the interdependence
of the seu and society and worked toward optimal and humane
relations between them. Although their primary audiences were
black communities, their choice and use of symbols, language, and
ideas strongly suggest that they self-consciously spoke to a wider
public.

Even in a patriarchal society, articulate black men have always
experienced enormous difficulties gaining recognition and "voice"
in the broader culture. This phenomenon of "invisibility," brilliantly
portrayed by novelist Ralph Ellison [*The Invisible Man*, 1952], has
weighed doubly hard upon black women. My study of four highly
visible, influential male leaders clearly signals the need for a cor-
responding study of black female (womanist) leaders. Already, this
task has been engaged by scholars such as Katie G. Cannon, Cheryl
Townsend Gilkes, Delores Williams, Cheryl J. Sanders, and others.
Until this historical and constructive work has been advanced adequately, our understanding of American social and moral thought
will remain inchoate.

Other studies of these figures have either ignored their reflections on individual morality and personal fulfillment or have dismissed these reflections as secondary to their broader strategies for
social change.[2] I deliberately emphasize the personal dimension of
their moral and social philosophies in this book. I intend to suggest
a more balanced reading and richer appreciation of their intellectual
and practical achievements and to call attention to a neglected insight
that informed their enterprises, namely, that meaningful societal
transformation entails and is bound up with personal transformation.

I wish to achieve four objectives here. First, I demonstrate that
each figure was a serious thinker whose reflections on morality and
justice merit additional scholarly attention. I maintain that inter-
pretations of their writings should continue, as such exploration
discloses depths and wisdom that premature closure has obscured.

Second, I show that their images of the authentically free person
are important and not trivial. These images represent different ways
in which blacks have sought to organize their individual and collective lives in the past hundred years. They are particularly significant because of the sociocultural context from which they

emerged. An appreciation of these images as synthetic cultural ideas forged from African, American, and European sources is long overdue. Understanding the critiques of American society and culture that their images of fulfillment advance or imply is also important.

Third, their conceptions of the authentic life and the just society are public and should not be construed to be isolated, exotic cultural artifacts, nor should they be restricted in their possible appeal to the black communities of North America. Indeed, each moralist enjoyed international respect. As intentional public thinkers, in differing degrees, they spoke to all of America and beyond as they pressed their claims for equal justice and opportunity. Their writings and speeches were public texts of their visions of a better community—visions that merit the attention and scrutiny of all intelligent people in a pluralistic marketplace of ideas.

Fourth, I hope to test the utility of contemporary moral philosophy for providing an analytic framework with which to organize and illumine the often-unsystematized insights of the black public moralists. The four thinkers I have selected to examine defy simple categorization and, hence, the need for a common framework. Beyond their generic similarity as well-known leaders, stark personal contrasts distinguish them. Washington was an educator and administrator; Du Bois, a social scientist and political propagandist; Malcolm, a sectarian religious spokesman and leader; and King, a professionally trained theologian, philosopher, and Christian pastor. Nevertheless, each of them engaged in a common enterprise of moral uplift and social reform that expanded beyond the seams of their vocational identities.

In order to portray accurately the thrust of their aspirations, I have chosen to characterize them as "public moralists."[3] This phrase, coined by journalist Peter Goldman, captures both the public and quasi-religious cast of national black leadership. Whatever their vocations, black leaders have at least functioned as religious leaders combining prophetic, priestly, messianic, pastoral, and other modes of guidance.

If we think of the four as moralists, categories from contemporary moral philosophy are an appropriate way to organize the wisdom tradition in black communities. I have chosen categories from the work of William Galston, a philosopher at the University of Texas (*Justice and the Human Good*), and John Rawls, the eminent Harvard philosopher (*A Theory of Justice*).[4] Both Galston and Rawls set forth theories of justice that impress me as congruent with the spirit and intent of the black leaders.

Specifically, Galston outlines four categories of allocable goods for which people and groups may make claims of entitlement: political goods (citizenship, political leadership), economic goods (income, property), goods of recognition (honor, status), and goods of personal development (education, culture). Also, he elaborates two types of valid claims that can be made for these goods: those based on need (when people lack the ensemble of means necessary for fulfilled existence) and desert (when they possess some quality that places them in a preferred position relative to some good).

John Rawls offers a modern version of the social contract theory of justice. It is founded upon two principles: political liberty and social-economic fairness. Rawls provides a mechanism for protecting the interests of the least-favored members of society (the difference principle) and thereby enhances the capacity for justice in his liberal theory.[5] He stipulates that the social order is not to establish and secure the more attractive prospects of those better-off unless doing so is to the advantage of those less fortunate. In this way, he links the fate of the poor to that of the well-off. The entire theory is problematic insofar as he accepts the inherent fairness of gross inequities within society. Nevertheless, the difference principle may be a useful analytic and normative mechanism for black leaders and others who seek to analyze and ultimately restructure American society.

Notwithstanding the possible methodological utility of such moral philosophical frameworks, their descriptive power is severely compromised by their limited attention to the cultural, racial, gender, and class factors that determine a person's or group's progress toward development and maturation. In other words, moral and social philosophies based on uncritical generalizations from the experience of privileged white males cannot claim descriptive adequacy or normative authority in communities of the oppressed.

Therefore, a mutually critical, theoretical exchange between contemporary moral philosophers and African-American religious and political thinkers is urgently needed. Black moralists can broaden the appeal of moral philosophy by correcting and expanding the perspective of such theorizing in a culturally pluralistic nation; academic philosophers can strengthen the efforts of the black moralists by helping to systematize black folk wisdom and render it accessible to a wider public.

In this book, each chapter contains four sections: a root metaphor; a biographical sketch; a conception of the moral life; and a conception of the just society. In selecting the root metaphors, I have attempted to discover, synthesize, or distill a pithy adjective or metaphor that best summarizes the image of fulfillment advanced by the moralist. Root metaphors emerge as responses to the central question with which the moralist seemed to be concerned during his life.

For Washington, the central question of his public career seemed to be, How might free blacks make steady progress toward full citizenship and economic independence in view of the realities of the slave past and of white racism? The root metaphor of his thought, I suggest, is the *adaptive life*.

Washington frequently urged free blacks to sacrifice certain moral goods (political rights) in the interest of more fundamental and less controversial nonmoral goods (wealth, property). The good person was one who, after making the correct utilitarian calculations, adapted to the exigencies of the given social context.

During Du Bois's long life, many questions occupied his protean imagination. A consistent concern seemed to be, How might blacks achieve personal wholeness and societal power without ignoring their cultural indebtedness to Africa, America, and Europe? The central metaphor that best characterizes his response is the *strenuous life*. As he diagnosed black life in America, he agonized over the inner fragmentation that underlie community disunity and impotence. Blacks were in need of self-merger, a complex, dialectical personal and communal process that would forge a new identity from complementary remnants of the past and present. The authentically free person was a rhythmically astute individual who vigorously pursued noble achievements while preserving the capacity to enjoy life's pleasures.

For Malcolm X, the central question seemed to be, How might blacks overcome the traumas of a multifaceted oppression and actualize community power and self-determination? The root metaphor I have chosen is the *defiant life*. Malcolm understood the logic of oppression to require the poor and nonwhite to be convinced of the moral legitimacy of inequality. Life was fundamentally conflict laden. In order to achieve a proud, black identity and religious, political, economic, and cultural self-reliance, the authentically free person must resist—defy the entire legitimation structure of white, Western superiority.

In the face of white negations of black identity and history, the defiant person responds with a resounding "No, never again!" and sets in motion a process of ongoing liberation for blacks and whites, Westerners and the Third World.

The central question for Martin Luther King, Jr., was, How might blacks discover, in the process of achieving equal justice, their fundamental identities as members of an interconnected, global human family? The root metaphor that captures his vision of authenticity is the *integrative life*. King understood all human life to be sacred and interdependent. All people are children of their common, personlike God. This fundamental moral commitment authorized the integrative person to resist and transform social institutions and practices that violated the sacred and relational aspects of human beings. The integrative person approaches fulfillment only as she or he integrates into her or his consciousness and identity the truths of other symbolic, cultural, and religious traditions. The integrative (rather than integrated) life is a process, not an achievement.

The brief biographical sketches reveal the effect of their formative years on their adult vocations. The sketches also serve to remind us of the different texture of each moralist's early life. Washington was born a slave and emerged a free voice for the black working class. Du Bois, the boy genius of New England, evolved into a lonesome warrior whose precocious solutions to the race question often produced mistrust and distance between himself and the masses. Malcolm X was nurtured by a proud, disciplined mother and a black nationalist father. Following the fragmentation of his family and his learning in the street and prison subcultures, he found wholeness outside black, Christian culture in his distinctive appropriation of Islam. Martin Luther King, Jr., was a childhood performer who recognized early his ability to move crowds emotionally. He emerged from a comfortable, middle-class Baptist home and years of intellectual preparation to become an advocate for the oppressed masses.

To some extent, the formative experiences of these figures are encapsulated in the root metaphors outlined above. However, I am reluctant to argue that the lives of these figures are adequately summarized by metaphors because their lives were more complex and dynamic than metaphors indicate. This qualified claim permits us to speak of Washington's adaptability, Du Bois's strenuousness, Malcolm X's defiance, and King's integrativeness.

In the third section of each chapter, I set out the moralist's understanding of the moral life. Making use of William Galston's categories of individual goods, I indicate the prominence of one or more of these goods in each moralist's thought. For Washington, economic goods were central. For Du Bois, political goods were essential for gaining access to the others. For Malcolm X, the goods of personal development made possible the attainment of economic and political goods. King balanced integration of all four categories.

In the final section of each chapter, I sketch the moralist's conception of the just society or at least what his conception might be if systematically elaborated. Washington envisioned a utopian, multiracial, conflict-free republic. Du Bois argued for the necessity of a democratic socialist political economy if blacks, other Americans, and indeed all humans were to achieve a just social existence. Malcolm X's view shifted from a racially separatist and capitalistic orientation to reflect his later commitments to a nonracial, democratic, socialist, and religiously pluralistic society. King envisioned a society in which democratic socialist ideals were established to secure equal justice for all. For him, however, the just society was not the highest social achievement available to humankind. People could be inspired and socialized to pursue the good, beloved society—a society in which Christian love functions to regulate mere rules of justice. Under these terms, the sacred and relational aspects of humankind could be affirmed.

I conclude the book by maintaining that King's vision of justice and fulfillment are, relative to the others, more public, monumental, and compelling. I defend this claim by demonstrating King's fidelity to certain fundamental sources that define the texture of black life, including black folk culture, prophetic Christianity, and American human rights traditions.

1

Booker T. Washington
and the Adaptive Person

One of the sharp dichotomies in American life divides people of thought from people of action. According to Louis R. Harlan, biographer and editor of Washington's papers, Washington was not an intellectual, but a man of action who used ideas as instruments to gain power. Harlan also warns that those who try to understand Washington in ideological terms as a realistic black philosopher or as an intellectual opposite of W. E. Burghardt Du Bois miss the essential character of the man.[1]

On one hand, Harlan's warning is justified. Washington never purported to be a philosopher. On the other hand, we would be unfair to dismiss Washington and his corpus of public writings, speeches, and letters as the collected thoughts of a black institution builder who lacked broad intellectual perspective and a morally serious vision of people and society. Moreover, the thought-action dichotomy characteristic of the dominant culture is far less pronounced, if at all relevant, in African-American intellectual history and culture. Historically, black intellectuals and scholars have been activists in movements for freedom and justice.

Within the imagination of this vigorous man of action existed a broad vision of the moral life and the just social order that guided his practical activities. Although not an intellectual when measured by modern Western canons, he was a thinking man who took his ideas seriously and with his actions made those ideas concrete.

Substantial data to support the claim that Booker T. Washington was a public moralist can be found in his Sunday evening talks to the Tuskegee student community. Washington preached and sought to embody the virtues of an authentically free life.

+ The Adaptive Person +

Washington developed the basis of a moral psychology of the "hand, head, and heart" with which he sought to guide the character formation and economic progress of black individuals and of the race.[2] The organizing vision or metaphor that unites the various threads of his thought may be characterized as the *adaptive person*. The adaptive person can satisfy the relevant achievement criteria in the areas of industrial (hand), intellectual (head), and moral (heart) development. The adaptive person should possess the requisite economic virtues with which he might contribute profitably to America's capitalistic economy. For Washington, moral virtues such as honesty seemed to derive their significance from the supportive function they provided for certain economic goods.

Washington seemed to embody the spirit of the metaphor in the following words:

> When I settled down for my life's work near the little town of Tuskegee, Alabama, I made up my mind to do as an individual that which I am striving to get my race to do throughout the United States. I resolved to make myself, so far as I was able, so useful to the community, the county, and the state that every man, woman, and child, white and black, would respect me and want me to live among them.[3]

As an adaptable, useful person, he would be an irresistible socioeconomic commodity who would contribute to the common good in society.

Note that *utility* is defined in relation to a social system, in this case, to the "community, county, and state." For Washington, the authentic person adapts to the environment and character of the local community. Conformity of this sort would lead to the social peace necessary for economic progress. As long as people contributed to the common good, they would be considered desirable, praiseworthy community members.

Apart from its inherently conservative cast, this style of reasoning is distinctly utilitarian. Acts and personal traits are judged good to the extent that they maximize the amount of desired goods without creating offsetting harm. Such conservative thinking authorized Washington to suggest that blacks forgo certain constitutionally guaranteed rights of citizenship in the immediate interest of preserving racial harmony. Adaptive blacks should help to create the cooperative context out of which economic progress would emerge. Thus, blacks were urged to consider economic instead of explicitly political means for supporting their claims for equal opportunity.

This was Washington's most controversial suggestion and perhaps his most ingenious strategy. He adopted a publicly passive posture with respect to political participation and social integration with whites and identified the economic marketplace as the meaningful arena in which blacks might advance their causes without arousing the suspicions of whites. In his published private papers, however, Washington provided financial support for political and legal efforts to strike down discriminatory legislation and to increase black voter strength across the South. As a man of his times, he argued and convinced many whites and blacks that the economic advance of the Negro, the "man farthest down," would result in the overall economic uplift of the southern region, a region preoccupied with reconstruction after a devastating war.

This strategy was controversial because it urged blacks to subsume their immediate political goals under long-term, economic benefits. With keen insight, Washington recognized that true power in America belonged to property owners and producers of consumer goods. This form of quiet power, wielded by farmers and small manufacturers, stood in marked contrast to the less predictable, symbolic power of the gifted black elite and radicals who held Washington in disdain. Nevertheless, in the face of opposition from the articulate and radical voices of Du Bois, Monroe Trotter, and the Niagara Movement, Washington maintained that economic self-reliance was the key to salvation for the black masses in America.

+ Biographical Sketch +

Booker T. Washington was the last of the major black leaders to be born in slavery. He was born on the farm of his owner, James

Burroughs, in the spring of 1856.[4] No one is certain about the identity of Washington's white father. Washington himself never knew him, except that he was someone of the neighborhood. "Whoever he was," said Washington, "I never heard of his taking the least interest in me or providing in any way for my rearing."[5] Without bitterness he observed that his father was "simply another unfortunate victim" of the institution of slavery.[6] His mother, Jane, worked as a cook on the farm and because her responsibilities were numerous, she had little time to nurse or care for him and his older brother, John. As soon as he had grown to sufficient size, Washington's task was that of fanning flies at mealtime in the master's house. According to biographer Louis Harlan, this allowed him to learn "something of table manners and mealtime conversation."[7]

After 1865, Jane and the children exercised their new freedom by moving to Malden, West Virginia, to join Jane's husband, Washington Ferguson (from whom Booker T. appropriated his own surname).[8]

Washington's adult teaching concerning economic self-reliance had its beginnings in his early experiences as a worker in the salt mines (with his stepfather) and as a houseboy. He worked as a houseboy for the leading family in Malden. General Lewis Ruffner and his wife, Viola, were fond of him despite his early difficulties in adjusting to her strict New England (Vermont) rules for cleanliness and order.

His first encounter with formal religious instruction occurred when he was reprimanded for playing marbles on Sunday morning by an old man who then led him to Sunday school. He began to attend regularly the African Zion Baptist Church in Tinkersville, as did his entire family.[9] Years later he advanced his studies at Hampton Institute in Hampton, Virginia.

At Hampton Institute, he developed a love of daily Bible reading and was impressed by the strong work ethic of the New England Protestant teachers and missionaries. At the age of twenty-two, during his phase of vocational searching, he attended Wayland Seminary in Washington, D.C., for one year, but grew dissatisfied with the formal academic character of the religious studies, which taught little in the way of practical arts for living. He expressed his disdain for the easy life of students at the Baptist seminary as compared with the hard experiences of Hampton students.

They seemed to give more attention to mere outward appearances. In a word, they did not appear to me to be beginning at the bottom, on a real, solid foundation, to the extent that they were at Hampton. They knew more about Latin and Greek when they left school, but they seemed to know less about life and its conditions as they would meet it at their homes.[10]

Washington abandoned his pursuit of the ministry and was invited to return to Hampton as a housefather of the Indian boys' dormitory.[11] Subsequently, his religious life seems to have been nurtured outside religious institutions and to have been influenced by the New England Unitarians with whom he interacted during his fund-raising efforts. By the time of his death in 1915, he had become thoroughly nonsectarian.[12]

During his time at Hampton Institute, he came under the influence of the principal, General Samuel Chapman Armstrong, who had been an advocate of black freedom and educational advance since his military service in the Union Army. The son of missionaries in Hawaii, Armstrong helped to establish Hampton as a place "to train selected Negro youths who should go out and teach and lead their people, first by example, by getting land and homes."[13] Washington's most meaningful experience of his first year was his contact with Armstrong. He wrote, "The first time I went into his presence he made the impression upon me of being a perfect man."[14] Harlan speculates that in Armstrong Washington found the white father figure he had perhaps unconsciously been seeking.[15] At Hampton, certainly, Washington came under the tutelage of a number of elite whites from New England who instilled in him a love of Bible reading, public speaking, common labor, and high moral character.[16]

Clearly, Washington's early life experiences brought him into continuous, close contact with whites. This contact permitted him the opportunity to observe, imitate, analyze, criticize, and empathize with their lifeways. More than any other black leader of the twentieth century, Washington knew the minds of southern white planters and of humiliated Confederate soldiers. Not only did he observe the socialization of white youth during his servant duties but he, too, was socialized into the distinct ethos of southern racial etiquette, economic independence, and mistrust of the North. This experience no doubt produced in young Washington a kinship consciousness with whites, a bond reinforced by the knowledge that his father was one of the local white men. I support Harlan's suggestion that General Armstrong became an idealized father figure for Washington. More importantly, as a house servant Washington experienced a model of racial cooperation in which blacks provided useful services for whites, whites rewarded blacks economically and allowed them exposure to higher material standards of living, and both races found security and order in the informal network of rules regulating contact between them. This early life experience as a houseboy, miner, and student of General Armstrong would later inform his mission in the fields of Tuskegee, Alabama.

Tuskegee Institute became the concrete embodiment of Washington's vision for black America. He should be given credit for establishing an institution designed to improve black life and American society. The Tuskegee achievement is especially noteworthy because it was a black institution in the South. Harlan notes that Tuskegee

> was an all-black school with an all black faculty at a time when most black colleges were still run by white missionaries. Tuskegee taught self-determination. It also taught trades designed for economic independence in a region dominated by sharecrop agriculture. At the same time, by verbal juggling tricks, Washington convinced the southern whites that Tuskegee was not educating black youth away from the farms. Tuskegee also functioned as a *model black community*, not only by acquainting its students with a middle class way of life, but by buying up the surrounding farmland and selling it at low rates of interest to create a community of small landowners and homeowners.[17] (Italics mine.)

Tuskegee functioned like a preparatory school by teaching blacks the requisite skills for participation in America's commercial life and enabling them to prove their accomplishments to a scrutinizing public. Washington and Tuskegee worked vigorously to fulfill General Armstrong's mission to "train selected Negro youths" to teach and lead their people by example. For many of the students and ex-slaves, it was a first, if modest, introduction to modern life.

Although he was the founder and president of the Institute, Washington taught courses on "Mental and Moral Science, Rhetoric, Grammar, and Composition."[18] Biographer Samuel R. Spencer, Jr., points out that Washington taught psychology to the senior class and there he enjoyed "his most intimate contact with students."[19] One youth wrote that in this class "the members of the senior class talk of their past and future lives and receive the outpourings of a great but simple soul."[20]

Washington was an architect of personality who wanted to place the final brick in position as he instructed his departing students (missionaries) in the arts of frugal, moral, civilized living and public communication. This would have followed years of study and work in industrial and agricultural science. At Tuskegee, students learned to live modestly but well and were expected to return to the farms and towns of the South in order to spread the gospel according to Washington.

In 1895 at a commercial exposition in Atlanta, Washington was selected to represent Negro achievements in a speech to the vast audience of whites and blacks. This memorable address succeeded in launching his career as a national public figure. In it, he urged whites to disregard black agitation for social equality while allowing, even encouraging, black economic advancement. He urged the black Southerners to remain in the region ("Cast down your buckets where you are") and to voluntarily segregate themselves from whites for the purpose of building an economically strong community.[21]

In subsequent years, Washington would become the chief black advisor to Presidents Theodore Roosevelt and William Howard Taft.[22] According to Harlan, Washington functioned like something of a machine boss in raising and channeling philanthropic monies to Tuskegee and other black institutions, securing federal jobs for his lieutenants, and sabotaging the tactics of his ideological and political opponents, especially Du Bois.

He was a man driven by his sense of his unique role in race relations. I would characterize this as a priestly performance in American public life. He sought to stand between the extremists in both races and to reconcile their interests by subsuming them under the broader general interest of prosperity and peace for the South and the nation.

If we are to assess Washington fairly, we must remember his context. It may help us to understand the tone and language of his public discourse. Washington's personal experience of slavery and proximity to whites forged an adaptive personality and a conciliatory agenda that may be inappropriate for our times. Nevertheless, modern readers should remember that Washington's ideas were situationally rational—he was a man of his time.

In the following sections, I organize and examine Washington's thought into a coherent vision of the moral life. I have limited my analysis to his public writings (books, articles, and speeches), as my purpose is to call attention to Washington as a moralist who spoke to a diverse American public. When information in his private correspondence illumines or contradicts his public statements, I have attempted to indicate this.

+ Conception of Human Fulfillment +

Let us now examine three of the concerns that were prominent in nearly all of Washington's public utterances: economic self-reliance, pragmatic religion, and education for noble vocations. As the leading Negro spokesman of the day, naturally he was concerned about a broader spectrum of social concerns, for example, an economic renaissance in the South, cautious black political empowerment and liberal arts and professional education. In this chapter I maintain that his broad vision of the moral life encompassed all of these concerns and can be adequately summarized by focusing on the three categories of economics, religion, and education.

In July 1884, Washington addressed the National Education Association and noted that southern whites were beginning to apprehend "the mighty truth that wealth, happiness, and permanent prosperity will only come in proportion as the hand, head, and heart of both races are educated and Christianized."[23] In an address before the Alabama State Teachers' Association on 11 April 1888, Washington proclaimed that "the perfect man is to come through a systematic and harmonious development of body, mind, and soul."[24]

In these comments Washington presents his wholistic vision of individual development. The moral person evolves toward maturity only insofar as he or she is challenged systematically to develop physically, intellectually, and spiritually. Education is the means by which such development is achieved. The end of this process should manifest itself in a productive, hardworking person who contributes to the "wealth, happiness, and permanent prosperity" of the society. He emphasized the ability and obligation of every person to become an economically resourceful, self-determining agent. Thus, the authentic person would be a laborer who possessed distinctive and refined agricultural or industrial skills and who could provide desired services in the local community.

Economic Self-Reliance

In an effort to promote his image of the authentic person as a fulfilled laborer, Washington found he had to rehabilitate the popular perception of labor as thoughtless, servile activity. On 18 November 1896, during an address at Hampton Institute, Washington explained that he was attempting to make the Negro "an intelligent, conscientious, skillful producer" and have him appreciate the "dignity, beauty, and civilizing power that is in labor."[25]

In the book *The Story of My Life and Work*, he stated, "As a race there are two things we must learn to do—one is to put brains into the common occupations of life, and the other is to dignify common labor."[26] Although some black elites may have found this rehabilitation effort humorous, Washington understood it to be essential to modern living. The black working class must be encouraged to apply scientific knowledge and methods to daily life, thereby rendering life more comfortable and efficient.

In an effort to dignify common labor, he had to dissociate the labor of free men and women and its virtues from the familiar forced, dehumanizing labor of the slave era. In 1907, he delivered two speeches on the economic development of the Negro race in slavery and since emancipation. They are contained in a book that, ironically, includes two lectures by W. E. B. Du Bois, who reflected on the economic revolution and religious practice in the South. In his second speech, Washington observed that "being worked meant degradation, working means civilization."[27] While drawing sharp contrast between slave and free labor, he began to advance his case for the ennobling effects of the Puritan work ethic. Laboring on some purposeful enterprise was not perceived to be mundane, thoughtless, alienated activity as it would come to be regarded following America's rapid industrialization after the First World War. Rather, non-factory and agricultural labor was thought to be a self-projecting, creative activity through which free, creative persons might express their self-esteem, intelligence and responsibility. Although he encouraged blacks to develop manufacturing skills, his principal concern was to advance agricultural productivity. This glorification of farming accounts for his somewhat naive conception of laborers as inherently noble and morally upright.

Another strategy for dignifying labor was illustrated by Washington's instrumental role in organizing and leading the National Negro Business League (1900). This group became the organizational base from which he proposed that race leadership should thereafter be supplied by a new elite class of black business people and entrepreneurs. Following his experiences at Wayland Seminary and Hampton, he placed greater confidence in the leadership potential of producers and managers than of preachers and politicians.

For him, the wealthy class of philanthropists and tycoons possessed the requisite virtues and resources needed to set the South, the black population, and, indeed, the nation on the course of progress. Julius Rosenwald served on Tuskegee's board of trustees in 1912, John D. Rockefeller was a major donor to Washington's dreams, and, through Washington, Andrew Carnegie gave libraries, dormitories, and other buildings to twenty-nine black schools.[28] In time, his affection for this elite overshadowed his devotion to the working class. Those who enjoyed enormous economic security and were civic-minded were better suited for public leadership.

At the first annual meeting of the National Negro Business League in Boston on 24 August 1900, he observed,

> Whether in the North or in the South, wherever I have seen a black man who was succeeding in business, who was a taxpayer, and who possessed intelligence and high character, that individual was treated with the highest respect by the members of the white race. In proportion as we can multiply these examples North and South will our problem be solved. Let every Negro strive to become the most useful and indispensable man in his community.[29]

He went on to catalogue the virtues he admired in black business owners.

> Every member of the race who succeeds in business, however humble and simple that business may be, because he has learned the important lessons of cleanliness, promptness, system, honesty, and progressiveness, is contributing his share in smoothing the pathway for this and succeeding generations.[30]

Moreover, he devoted an entire book, *The Negro in Business* (1907), to elaborating in painstaking detail the economic achievements of individual blacks.[31] Washington's fundamental image of the authentically free person was the hardworking, independent laborer capable of balancing personal interests with the needs of the wider community.

Drawing upon his distinction between free and servile labor, Washington believed that achieving an authentic moral life entailed more than mere employment. Rather, persons needed vocations. On 11 April 1888 at the Alabama State Teachers Association, Washington insisted that "every youth should be helped to find what God meant for him to do."[32] As he understood vocation, individuals were called by the deity both to discover their innate aptitudes and purposes and to work diligently in them. Fulfillment lay not so much in experiencing happiness in the carrying out of one's vocation as much as knowing that one was doing what God had purposed for him or her and that this labor served ultimately to create a better community. In this context, the industrial school was the primary institution responsible for helping youths to identify their vocations. No wonder Washington became personally involved in the instructional life of the school through his Sunday evening talks and through teaching the senior class.

The notion of fulfillment through vocation represented a significant intellectual and strategic option to the position of Du Bois. Whereas Du Bois conceived of fulfillment in terms of political empowerment and scholastic excellence, Washington saw possibilities for self-actualization largely independent of the political realm. As he surveyed the condition of the southern black masses following the demise of Reconstruction, he was convinced that all were not ready for full political responsibility. He thought that the poor or irresponsible exercise of political rights might produce resentment among whites and thereby hurt the cause of racial uplift. Yet, as he learned in 1895, these same whites could be persuaded to allow black economic advances within certain limits.

As we have seen, Washington's vision of the authentically free person emphasized vocation, the Puritan work ethic, and the virtues associated with adapting personal interests to community needs. Let us now consider his case for the priority of economic goods in the authentic life.

Always aware of the criticism his social philosophy would meet, frequently he put forth his economic agenda in defensive terms. "[I] didn't seek to give the people the idea that political rights were

not valuable or necessary but that *economic efficiency is the foundation for every kind of success*"[33] (italics mine). The next quotation
provides evidence for my claim that he understood economic goods
to be essential for living an authentically free life.

> I would set no limits to the attainments of the Negro in arts, in
> letters or statesmanship, but I believe the surest way to reach
> those ends is by laying the foundation in the little things of life
> that lie immediately about one's door. I plead for industrial edu-
> cation and development for the Negro not because I want to cramp
> him, but because I want to free him. I want to see him enter the
> all-powerful business and commercial world.[34]

For Washington, secure freedom rested upon controlling material assets, especially land, small businesses, and homes. Achievements in the arts, politics, and other more refined, nonmaterial
endeavors were praiseworthy only if they were buttressed by an
economic power base and community self-determination. Blacks
who possessed abundant artistic and political skills without economic
power resembled the powerless, entertaining Negro minstrels who
depended on the good favor of whites for their livelihood.

Authentic liberation required that the black community establish itself on a relatively self-sufficient economic basis, produce for
itself all that it needed to live, and produce certain consumer items
of such high quality that whites and others would support the items
in the marketplace. Only after achieving economic self-reliance
would other nonmaterial goods and values (arts, civic debate) come
to have utility and meaning for the black community.

Washington's convictions concerning the economic foundations
of authentic liberation were, and continue to be, compelling. As the
waning years of the twentieth century approach, many black communities find themselves struggling to realize Washingtonian proposals concerning the need for strong black businesses and revalorizing common labor, the work ethic, and vocation as divinely
sanctioned. Despite the attractiveness of many of his ideas, however,
they have been compromised by numerous historical factors.

Professor John Hope Franklin observes that the weaknesses of
"the Washington formula" for black economic liberation are more
obvious today than they were during Washington's era.[35] First, Washington's "doctrine of triumphant commercialism" was flawed insofar
as he accepted uncritically the dominant philosophy of American

business, which held that every person had his future in his own hands.[36] Recall that Washington organized the National Negro Business League supposing that those who could manufacture a better consumer item and sell it cheaper could also command the marketplace. In his second, more famous autobiography, *Up From Slavery* (1901), he noted Tuskegee's success in selling bricks to local whites who were previously hostile to the idea of a black school in the community.[37] He observed that

> any individual who learned to do something better than anybody else—learned to do a common thing in an uncommon manner— and that in proportion as the Negro learned to produce what other people wanted and must have, in the same proportion would he be respected.[38]

Other critics of Washington's formula have noted that this philosophy was an adaptation of the theories of free competition and political individualism that had been taught by the school of classical political economy and were becoming more fictitious than ever before by 1900.[39]

Second, Washington can be criticized for articulating a brand of industrial education that was "outmoded at the time he enunciated it, by the increasing industrialization of the country."[40] His failure to grasp the effects of the Industrial Revolution led him to urge blacks to prepare for farm-oriented occupations and vocations in brickmasonry and carpentry, which were then diminishing. Harlan is more judicious in his appraisal of Washington's formula on this point. He notes that the formula was anachronistic for the age of mass production, but "it had considerable social realism for a black population which was, until long after Washington's death, predominantly rural and southern. Furthermore, it was well attuned to the growth and changing character of black business in his day."[41] The market to which black businesses catered was then beginning to shift away from whites to urban blacks. Black solidarity then emerged as a matter of economic as well as political and cultural concern.[42]

Third, Washington vigorously opposed the massive black migration from the South into northern urban centers and urged blacks to remain in rural areas. Franklin reckons that Washington failed to see that "the advent of expensive farm machinery put the impoverished Negro at a serious disadvantage" and that "the industrial urban community was infinitely more attractive to Negroes as well as to whites."[43] Following the Civil War and Reconstruction period, many blacks felt the need to test their freedom by leaving the South. Others fled in pursuit of economic, cultural, and intellectual opportunities for growth. Few of them were inclined to give heed to the cry, "Cast down your buckets where you are."

To a certain extent, Washington's critics are correct. His sanguine view of capitalism, his pre-Industrial Revolution educational program, and his pro-rural vision compromised the subsequent utility of his answer to the question of black liberation. He was a man of his times, and times were changing rapidly even as he spoke. In other respects, nevertheless, he was an exceedingly perceptive and sensitive leader. He perceived the important psychological prerequisites to entering American public life. Like the European immigrants, in the course of struggling to survive economically blacks would discover and cultivate the necessary virtues for wielding power in both commercial and civic life. Owning property taught people about thrift, frugality, determination, planning and forecasting, delayed gratification, investing, and patience—virtues that might not be learned by perpetually working for others. If blacks would be good citizens and workers, they must learn living habits appropriate for free persons, such as thinking of the land as theirs and encouraging gifted family members to achieve and thereafter uplift the rest of the family, practices discouraged in the slave system. Blacks who migrated to northern cities were inadvertently leaving behind a land upon which they had developed entitlement claims by virtue of centuries of unpaid labor. In these teachings, Washington provided blacks with basic lessons in a protracted "introduction to modernity."

In *My Life and Work*, he explained, "I am no politician, on the other hand, I have always advised my race to give attention to acquiring property, intelligence, and character, as the necessary bases of good citizenship, rather than to mere political agitation."[44] Perhaps more than Du Bois, he apprehended the immediate psychic transformation that blacks must undergo in order to participate fully in the new century of growth.

Pragmatic Religion

Religiously, Washington was a complex man. Reared a Baptist, during the course of his life he drifted into the more liberal waters of Unitarianism. When he stood in the presence of black Baptists, however, he knew how to use the persuasive language and cadences of a preacher. This observation illumines the reason he at once embraced and rejected certain elements of African-American Christianity.

Washington realized that religion had historically been a fundamental element of southern and black cultural life. He was displeased by the explosively emotional and superstitious character of southern folk religion. However, he would have been foolhardy to deny or minimize the significance of religion in the South's future. Consequently, he offered an alternative model of being religious. His normative sketch of a more practical and lean religious faith and his style of evangelizing for it caused palpable tensions with the established black clergy.

Washington's understanding of the function of pragmatic religion is illustrated in the following passages:

> I may be accused of wrong interpretation, but when the Bible says, "Work out our salvation with fear and trembling," I am tempted to believe that it means what it says. In the past we have had the fear and trembling. As a race I believe we are to work out our salvation, work it out with pen and ink, work it out with rule and compass, work it out with horsepower and steam power, work it out on the farm, in the shop, school room . . . and in all life's callings. . . . I believe that we have a movement today that means salvation of the Negro race, and as my people are taught in these classrooms . . . *to mix up with their religion zeal and habits of thrift*, economy, carpentry . . . then as this influence penetrates the hills and valleys . . . we shall agree that it is most possible for a race as for an individual to actually work out its salvation.[45] (Italics mine.)
>
> In a moral and religious sense, while we admit there is much laxness in morals and superstition in religion, yet we feel that much progress has been made, that there is a growing public sentiment in favor of purity, and that the people are fast coming to make their religion less of superstition and emotion and more of a matter of daily living.[46]

Normatively, Washington conceived religion proper to be a set of divinely inspired motivations, attitudes, virtues, and rules. The function of practical religion was to provide for the ethical regulation of daily life. This could be done without myths, displays of emotion, and abstractions. Indeed, the value of practical religion, in contrast to the theological abstractions he encountered in Wayland Seminary and the folk superstitions of the country, resided precisely in its simple, direct, and tangible influence on everyday life, particularly economic life.

Given this narrow definition of religion as the moral influence on behavior, Washington's image of the authentic life permitted, even required, a mutually supportive relationship between religion and economic activity. Washington implied that religion alone was insufficient to adequately order one's life. He recalled that slave religion had enabled blacks to adapt to and survive horrific living conditions, but the means of adapting were excessively emotional, otherworldly, and inappropriate to free existence in a world that now belonged, in part, to the former slaves. The liturgical and ideational remnants of slave religion (shouting, dancing, hoodoo) tended to overemphasize supernatural, nonempirical realities and to demand a level of commitment that left little interest or energy for acquiring material goods. Consequently, slave religion had to be replaced by pragmatic religion in order to equip blacks for the modern world.[47]

Pragmatic religion would enable blacks to affirm—rather than deny—life in this world and thereby encourage their efforts to multiply their material holdings. Pragmatic religion, as he conceived it, was designed for free people with callings to fulfill. It was to be a working person's faith, thoroughly demythologized and cleansed of the excesses of Protestant evangelical revivalism.

Despite the changes in black religious life that he advocated, Washington embraced the black church, Bible reading, and singing Negro spirituals and affirmed his spiritual continuity with his roots in the African Zion Baptist Church. Historian Sydney Ahlstrom observes that although the adult Washington was not a churchman himself, he "accepted and strengthened the virtues, strategies and socio-political arrangements which nearly all the major Negro denominations and sects . . . then accepted—and which they by and large continued to accept down to World War II, and even after."[48] Ahlstrom fails to note, however, the condition by virtue of which Washington supported the churches, namely, their support for a modernized vision of group and personal fulfillment. In *The Story of the Negro*, he explained his position as follows:

> In my opinion, there is no other place in which the Negro race can to better advantage begin to learn the lessons of self-direction

and self-control than in the Negro church. I say this for the reason that in spite of the fact that other interests have from time to time found shelter there, *the chief aim of the Negro Church*, as of other branches of the Christian Church, has been *to teach its members the fundamental things of life and create in them a desire and enthusiasm for a higher and better existence here and hereafter.*[49] (Italics mine.)

Clearly, if the "chief aim" of the black churches had been contrary to Washington's moral and social program, he might have ignored them. Inasmuch as the churches functioned as classrooms or seminars in which black individuals learned self-determination, economic independence and civility, however, his pragmatic sensibilities urged him to cooperate with these centers of instruction and socialization into modern life. Washington also made efforts to fortify the life and mission of black churches by establishing a school at Tuskegee for training black preachers.

On 16 August 1907, Washington told a Hampton Institute audience that "no man's life is really complete until he owns a Bible that is part of himself."[50] While at Hampton, two New England teachers, Nathalie Lord and Elizabeth Brewer, insisted that he read the Bible daily.[51] In *Up From Slavery*, Washington testified,

> Perhaps the most valuable thing I got out of my second year [at Hampton] was an understanding of the use and value of the Bible. Before this I never cared a great deal about it, but now I learned to love to read the Bible, not only for the spiritual help which it gives, but on account of it as literature.[52]

Indeed, a visit to Tuskegee Institute confirms his conviction that the Bible's teachings and stories should shape the adaptive person's life. On the dormitory desks and in other places on campus are displayed moralisms and Bible passages to inspire better lives. Clearly, the Bible as a spiritual and literary classic held a central place in his conception of the adaptive life.

With respect to singing the spirituals, he said, "I would rather hear the jubilee or plantation songs of my race than the finest chorus from the works of Handel or any other of the great composers that I have heard."[53] He goes on to explain that

> through these songs the slaves found a means of telling what was in their hearts when almost every other means of expressing their thoughts and feelings was denied them. For this reason, if for no other, they will always remain a sacred heritage of the Negro race.[54]

He understood very well the therapeutic, political, and spiritual significance of the sorrow songs on which he was nurtured in black culture. As a spokesman for the race, he had to love the spirituals because they were living expressions of the souls of black folk. However, he also claimed for them a classic status. The depth and power of these human creations possessed broader, perhaps universal appeal. "My knowledge of the Negro has led me to believe that there is much in the story of his struggle, if one were able to tell it as it deserves to be told, that it is likely to be both instructive and helpful, not merely to the black man but also to the white man."[55] Similar to the biblical record of Jewish struggle and progress, the spirituals constituted a partial oral history of blacks who had marched from slavery to freedom. Thus, as history and as therapy, black sacred music would continue to be an important part of an authentically free life.

During the course of his public efforts to gain acceptance of this pragmatic religious faith, Washington often clashed with the established black clergy. Although he was a frequent speaker at some of the largest annual gatherings of black clergy and Christians, especially the National Baptist Convention, he blamed them for the material and spiritual underdevelopment of the masses. Often he seemed to pick fights with them.

At Fisk University's commencement in 1890, he verbally roasted black preachers as men unfit to lead the race.[56] His comments ignited a controversy that attracted wide attention to himself from blacks outside the educational field. Later, he published the speech under the title, "The Colored Ministry: Its Defects and Needs."[57] He began by arguing, courageously, that two-thirds of black ministers cared nothing for the moral or intellectual elevation of their people and were interested only in collecting their salaries. This attitude was the result of failing to train them properly. He observed that only a handful graduated each year from seminaries, and a large portion of these were Congregational, Episcopal or Presbyterian, whereas most blacks were Baptists or Methodists. He found black ministers in mainline white denominations to be "as a rule, intelligent and earnest," but out of touch with the black masses.[58] As for other black ministers, he said, "I have no hesitancy in asserting that three-fourths of the Baptist ministers and two-thirds of the Methodists are unfit, either mentally or morally, or both, to preach the Gospel to any one or attempt to lead any one."[59] As he saw it, these preachers perpetuated the nonprogressive features of slave religion. After diagnosing the illness of leadership in black churches, he offered a prescription for health.

He proposed a Bible training school "on a thoroughly Christian but strictly undenominational basis" to prepare a minister to read the Bible, prepare a sermon, sing a hymn, and use his calling to help the people.[60] Washington built Phelps Hall, a nonsectarian chapel on Tuskegee's campus that also housed the Phelps Hall Bible Training School for the elementary education of ministers. Given the controversy and the founding of the school, we could safely conclude that Washington criticized the clergy because he cared deeply for them and recognized the latent power that could be mobilized if leaders were properly educated.

Biographer Louis Harlan suggests that Washington may have attacked black clergy and founded a nondenominational Bible school in a calculated effort to "appeal to the Unitarians and Congregationalists in the North who were his chief philanthropic allies."[61] For a decade he had been plagued by rumors that he was a Unitarian and that Tuskegee was a Unitarian school. These rumors were fueled by the fact that one of his closest advisors, General J. F. B. Marshall, was a leading Unitarian and an officer of the American Unitarian Association. I agree with Harlan's observation that "it is probably true that Washington was influenced by the Unitarians who were kind to him."[62] Harlan goes on to express what I characterize as Washington's evolving eclectic religious identity.

> His approach to most matters was so pragmatic that he was capable of being a Unitarian among Unitarians, a Baptist among Baptists, and a doubter among skeptics. When his primary function was to raise money in New England churches, he did not stress his Baptist faith, but in the 1890s, when he sought to become a black leader, he gave emphasis to his membership in the largest black denomination.[63]

Washington's appropriation of Unitarianism buttressed the vision of pragmatic religion that he believed would produce measurable, material effects. In the Unitarian worldview, he discovered a flexible, nondogmatic theological system, an activist concern for social change and justice, and a clear, straightforward understanding of each person's moral obligation. These elements enabled him to appeal on a religious basis to white and black Christians to rectify the condition of the former slaves without becoming entangled in doctrinal disputations. His black Baptist worldview provided him with pastoral insight into the therapeutic and hope-engendering elements of slave religion, especially the spirituals. By integrating the two religious traditions that appealed to him, Washington forged a lean, practical faith option well-suited both to his need for personal renewal and to the needs of the masses. In the end, the chief test of good religion he proposed lay in its capacity to order daily life toward the end of achieving economic self-reliance.

Education for Vocation

> If education is of any practical value it should serve to guide us in living, in other words, *to fit us for the work around us* and demanded by the times in which we live. It should aid us in putting the most into life in the age, country, and into the *position we are to fill.*
>
> Perhaps all of us agree that that training is best which gives the student the broadest and most complete knowledge of the arts, sciences, and literature of all the civilized nations, ancient or modern, but where the want of time and money prevents this broader culture (and a choice must be made by most), let us choose to give the student that training in his own language, in the arts and sciences that will have special bearing on his life and will thus *enable him to render the most acceptable worship to God and the best service to man.*[64] (Italics mine.)

This quotation shows that Washington acknowledged the appropriateness of higher education in the arts and sciences of ancient and modern civilization. Portraying him as the ideological foe of Du Bois and others in regard to the merits of higher education versus industrial education is a mistake. Du Bois recognized the need for industrial training and a class of black artisans; Washington was a trustee of two of the leading black universities, Fisk and Howard. Both men acknowledged the significance of each.[65]

Ironically, at the same time Washington was considered an enemy by many black college graduates, he brought large sums of philanthropic money into need areas at every level of black education. To be sure, he took care of the needs of Tuskegee first, but he also helped to channel northern monies into a great number and variety of black higher educational institutions. Harlan notes, "As a dispenser of the philanthrophy of Andrew Carnegie and as a trustee of both Fisk University and Howard University he showed himself to be a friend rather than an enemy of black higher education."[66] Also, we should note that Washington's judgment that industrial education be provided for those who were for the moment unable to pursue higher education was prudent and situationally rational.

An ideal education for the adaptive person entailed three dimensions: personal, social, and religious. The personal dimension was designed to instill moral virtues and to cultivate reason, self-control, pride, and excellent performance in one's vocation. The social dimension was designed to cultivate a sense of moral obligation and responsibility for the common good. The religious dimension carried the responsibility of affirming the person as a finite creature whose potential greatness derived from relatedness to God. Working in concert, these dimensions would enable the adaptive person to find fulfillment as he or she demonstrated superior performance in his or her calling while accepting the burdens and benefits of being a member of a community and acknowledging his or her ultimate dependence on God.

With respect to the personal dimension, Washington said,

> Is the acquiring of reading, writing, and arithmetic education, or do these comprise the great results we seek for in education? These are education so far as they serve as stepping stones to the rich goal which we seek, but they are not all of education.
>
> Is the ability to master and converse in foreign languages, to travel through the wonderful intracacies of geometry and trigonometry education or the end we seek for? No, they are but the means to an end . . . nor shall the end be reached till every passion, every appetite be controlled, every prejudice, all malice, all jealousy be banished from the heart and every faculty of the mind be so governed that *the united and harmonious action of body, mind, and heart shall lead us up till we live in that atmosphere where God dwells.*[67] (Italics mine.)

Toward the end of realizing authentic freedom, Washington's educational philosophy placed heavy emphasis on the "step stones" of subduing passions, cultivating personal moral pur' fining rational thinking, and encouraging diligence in v pursuits.

Like Armstrong, Washington abhorred ignorance, drunkenness, poverty, and apathy. These and other obstacles to personal development were remediable if people would submit their appetites to the governance of reason. This mistrust of lower passions was typical of Puritanism and was derived from the educational ethos of New England Puritanism, with which he was much enamored. His studies with General Armstrong and the Hampton faculty and his association with New England leaders of business, religion, and education reinforced this style of moral education.

Washington knew that during slavery many passions and nonproductive behaviors went unrestrained. Personally, he was disgusted with the manner in which less pious slaves spent their occasional evening off in dancing, drinking, and promiscuous sexual play, behavior learned from and encouraged by many white slave holders. His mission was to apply to these excesses the corrective force of education in a controlled environment like Tuskegee so that reason would triumph over passion and people would be freed to pursue their callings.

Education was not to serve as an avenue for individual gratification or a passage for mobility away from one's community. Rather, it should instill a sense of social connectedness to others that would manifest itself in serving the least advantaged members of the community. He applied this logic both within the black community and in larger public arenas as he sought to counteract the raging, unproductive regional tensions active at the turn of the twentieth century. In a speech to the Hamilton Club in Chicago, he explained,

> Nor are we of the black race leaving the work alone to your race in the North or your race in the South—mark what this new citizen is doing. Go with me tonight to the Tuskegee Institute . . . in an old plantation where a few years ago my people were bought and sold, and I will show you an industrial village with nearly eight hundred young men and women working with head and hand preparing themselves, in literature, in science, in agriculture, in the duties of Christian citizenship . . . *preparing themselves that they may prepare thousands of others of our race that they may contribute their full quota of virtue*, of thrift and intelligence to the prosperity of our beloved country.[68] (Italics mine.)

As we have noted before, the missionary ethic of Tuskegee, which he appropriated from Hampton and Armstrong, authorized him to commission graduates to go forth and teach and lead their people into a better life. Du Bois referred to this cadre of educated black missionaries as the "talented tenth." Both moralists espoused a strong principle of communal responsibility within the black community, a significant effort to prevent the development of deep divisions within the black community based on class, culture, and color.

In this quote, Washington applies the logic of social connectedness and his vision of the common good in appealing to the noblesse oblige of northern whites. He believed that the industrialized North should assist the South in its reconstruction and that white leaders and citizens of both regions should join hands to improve the lot of the Negro. He understood keenly the post–Civil War tensions between southern and northern whites and in his shrewd, inimitable manner sought to position himself (and black America) between the two. From that position, he could extend olive branches to both sides by appealing to his vision of a prosperous, unified nation. Indeed, he believed that the labor, suffering, and sacrifices of blacks qualified them to teach others the "duties of Christian citizenship." Thus, he envisioned national unity emerging as whites and blacks overcame their prejudices and began to cooperate— although not integrate socially—with each other.

The final dimension of his understanding of education possessed a religious intent, namely, that reason be a part of the pragmatic religious faith discussed earlier. Consistently, he affirmed the presence of God in creation, nature, and history. Throughout his speeches Washington affirmed that God dispensed vocations and their concomitant faculties, aptitudes, and virtues, that God had sustained the slaves in their passage to freedom, and that God allowed the freedmen to experience challenges and chastening because God loved them.[69] A proper education should reinforce this God-consciousness without revalorizing the emotionalism and superstitions of slave religion. Thus, education should refine faith by enabling the adaptive person to reflect critically on the nature and effects of her or his religion.

Having examined his vision of human fulfillment, the adaptive life, let us now consider his reflections on the just society that, in most instances, can be inferred from his comments on human fulfillment.

+ The Just Society +

At this point, I wish to examine briefly Washington's understanding of the just society. First, I describe his modest utopian
vision of America. Next, I characterize his vision as a noncritical,
conservative one that reinforced the hegemony of white, Anglo-
Saxon, New England, Puritan culture. Finally, I sketch the reparations claims he advanced for economic justice.

Referring back to the theoretical framework sketched in the
introduction, I wish to consider Washington's views in light of William Galston's moral philosophical categories. Galston explains that
"utopian thought is the political branch of moral philosophy" and
that among its many functions it guides our deliberation in devising
courses of action, justifies our actions so that the grounds of action
are reasons that others ought to accept, and serves as the basis for
the evaluation of existing institutions and practices.[70] He goes on to
observe that utopian thought is characterized by its attempt to "spec-
ify and justify the principles of a comprehensively good political
order."[71] Utopian thought contains principles that are in their intention universally valid both temporally and geographically, and
the contradictions of experience may be imaginatively reconciled
and transmuted. Utopias exist in speech and as such are "cities of
words." The practical intention of utopia requires that it be constrained by possibility; although utopia is a guide for action, it is
not in any simple sense a program of action.[72] I find Galston's discussion suggestive for illumining quasi-utopian dimensions of Washington's discourse.

In his wide-ranging speeches, occasionally Washington acknowledged the motivational importance of an ideal standard for
societies and individuals. In a speech delivered before the Brooklyn
Institute of Arts and Sciences in 1903, he argued that "every government, like every individual, must have a standard of perfection
that is immovable, unchangeable, applicable to all races, rich and
poor, black and white, towards which its people must continually
strive."[73] He had just posited that the Ten Commandments and the
Golden Rule were examples of such standards. This position provides
support for my contention that Washington employed language and
symbols in support of a quasi-utopian vision of the just society. By
couching his vision in seemingly harmless, imaginative terms, he

managed to engage in a veiled form of political discourse designed
to mobilize the good will of white Americans, advance the status
and material power of black Americans, and strengthen the unity
of the American republic.

He believed that "standards of perfection" such as the Golden
Rule should guide the policies and actions of governments. If governments would conform to such noble ideals, they would foster the
emergence of just societies. Washington's remarks imply that the
standard would serve as the basis for evaluating existing government
actions and constantly highlighting discrepancies between the actual
and the intended state of things.

One of the best examples of his utopian imagination is illustrated
in this passage from a speech he delivered in 1896 titled, "Our New
Citizen":

> Let the Negro, the North, and the South do their duty with a
> new spirit and a new determination during this, the dawning of
> a new century, and at the end of fifty years a picture will be
> painted—what is it? A new race dragged from its native land in
> chains, three hundred years of slavery, years of fratricidal war,
> thousands of lives laid down, freedom for the slave, reconstruction,
> blunders, bitterness between North and South. The South staggers
> under the burden; the North forgets the past and comes to the
> rescue; the Negro, in the midst, teaching North and South pa-
> tience, forebearance, longsuffering, obedience to law, developing
> in intellect, character and property, skill and habits of industry.
> The North and South, joining hands with the Negro take him
> whom they have wronged, help him, encourage him, stimulate
> him in self-help, *give him the rights of man*, and, in lifting up the
> Negro, lift themselves up into that atmosphere where there is a
> new North, a new South—a new citizen—*a new republic*.[74] (Italics
> mine.)

The core conviction underlying this vision is quite significant,
namely, that the common good would be an outgrowth of uplifting
the least advantaged members of the community. For Washington,
national unity could be purchased only by rectifying the plight of
blacks. This unity would be the result of obedience to moral duties
to improve the lot of the disadvantaged and the result of a new
twentieth-century progressive outlook that should render antiquated
old racial practices. I call attention to the phrase, "give him [the
Negro] the rights of man." In a shrewd, unthreatening, futuristic

context, he advanced a detailed conception of what blacks would contribute to this new republic and what they would merit in return. At some undetermined point in the future (perhaps fifty years), blacks should receive full citizenship rights and responsibilities and thereby create a new republic.

Galston's sketch of the tasks of utopian thought offers a new perspective for assessing the degree of complexity and nuance in Washington's public philosophy. Washington imaginatively projected a new pattern of race relations portraying whites in the South and North "joining hands with the Negro" to lift the country to its intended status as a democratic republic. He did not allow the bleakness of the nation's slave past or his own personal history to circumscribe the possibilities for an optimistic future. Indeed, his vision was a "city of words." However, the picture was constrained by possibility in that its realization was contingent on responsible moral agency in the present.

Washington employed such visions in his public rhetoric without controversy. This demonstrates not only that he was an exceedingly credible and popular black voice in white America but also that his thought occasionally functioned at several levels. At the manifest level, with these visions he inspired whites in the South and North to at least consider benevolently the potential contribution of blacks as all Americans joined forces to build a strong, unified nation. At a latent level, he invited whites to imagine a day when blacks would claim deservedly the rights and responsibilities of citizenship and the nation would prove to be the ultimate beneficiary for having changed. In assessing his leadership, we must credit him with the achievement of inviting, and thereby preparing, segments of white America for full black political empowerment. In this light, we could conclude that Washington prepared the way for the uncompromising demands advanced by Du Bois and others.

Our second concern is to illustrate the uncritical, conservative character of his vision of the just society. By embracing America's form of government and by urging blacks to assimilate its values, he helped to preserve the hegemony of white, Anglo-Saxon, Protestant culture.

> Our republic is the outgrowth of the desire for liberty that is natural
> in every human breast—freedom of body, mind, and soul, and

the most complete guarantee of the safety of life and property.
. . . I need not take your time to remind you how, under the
leadership of George Washington, the result [of the American
Revolution] sought for was secured through the Declaration of
Independence, through Lexington, Concord, and Yorktown.[75]
(Italics mine.)

In statements such as this, Washington placed himself squarely
in the American Enlightenment tradition as he espoused Jeffersonian
ideals concerning human nature and "natural" forms of government.
Again, by including blacks in the category of those who possess a
natural desire for liberty, and by linking them to America's political
classics, in a nonthreatening and persuasive manner he advocated
full citizenship for blacks.

This conviction regarding the human's natural desire for liberty
has been usefully abstracted and reformulated into a broad principle
of social justice by moral philosopher John Rawls. Rawls's recasting
of Jeffersonian ideals takes the form of two basic principles of justice.
These principles, he argues, are ones that would be chosen by
persons in the hypothetical construct he refers to as the "original
position." By reading Washington in light of Rawls, I wish to suggest
that although Washington is a conservative social thinker, he stands
squarely in the American tradition of bourgeois individualism, especially its emphasis on protecting the economic rights of the individual. Rawls systematically elaborates convictions concerning the
inviolability of basic human and political rights that are usually and
deliberately implicit in Washington's rhetoric. Rawls suggests,

> First: each person is to have an equal right to the most extensive
> basic liberty compatible with a similar liberty for others.
>   Second: social and economic inequalities are to be arranged
> so that they are both (a) reasonably expected to be to everyone's
> advantage, and (b) attached to positions and offices open to all.[76]

From a substantive point of view, Rawls's principles are congruent with the core values of Washington's social philosophy. Both
assert the moral superiority of social arrangements that protect individual liberties and willingly assume reasonable burdens in order
to empower disadvantaged citizens to develop their potential. Rawls
notes that basic liberties include the right to vote, eligibility for
public office, freedom of speech, and freedom to hold property.[77]
Quietly, Washington embraced all of these.

Both thinkers recognize the necessity of moderating individual liberties by appealing to the larger community's needs. The fabric of society is delicate and cannot consistently bear the tug of selfish persons or interest groups, hence, the importance of the notion "compatible liberties." The adaptive person in Washington's thought possesses the other-regarding sensibilities that enable him to assess the compatibility of competing individual liberties.

Also, both thinkers accept the moral legitimacy of a social system containing obvious and inevitable economic inequality. Washington's elitism was most undisguised when expressing faith in entrepreneurs and wealthy people as the natural leaders of society. He was not troubled by the prospect of dramatic discrepancies in the control of wealth in society as long as the affluent made tangible efforts to improve the economic health of the working poor. Both are concerned that the social positions of affluent or impoverished citizens be open to all persons rather than a function of membership in a class. We may infer that they believe one's ultimate social position is in the hands of the individual. Other things equal, the ingenious rise to the top to the benefit of themselves and the rest of society.

To rehabilitate Washington's thought for the contemporary situation, therefore, one useful method would be to correlate these and other points of congruence he shares with Rawls's theory of justice.

The value of such potential dialogue would surely be mutual. Whereas Rawls helps to organize and elaborate implicit elements of Washington's social philosophy, Washington's personal experience and historical perspective as a former slave may broaden Rawls's empirical data base and enable him to consider systematically the unique psychosocial predicament of people who were enslaved and who continue to be maliciously denied the provisions he advocates. This underscores one of the principal limitations of traditional moral philosophy, its tendency to treat as normative the life experience and prospects of those who already possess a secure identity and sense of selfhood. This achievement cannot be assumed for former slaves. Consequently, their special historical experience must be reckoned with in developing theories of justice that are inclusive and true to the complex nature of past social relations in diverse societies.

Nevertheless, insofar as both thinkers take seriously the innate human desire for liberty and other American Enlightenment ideals such as freedom of speech and religious expression and private property, both thinkers should be understood to be translators of the American dream.

By urging blacks to assimilate the cultural habits and values of whites, Washington reinforced the cultural and political hegemony of white, Anglo-Saxon New England Puritanism. He viewed the imitation of white behavior and attitudes essential for black progress in a technological age.

Speaking to a Harvard Alumni Dinner on 24 June 1896, he affirmed the preeminence of the values of the persons seated before him.

> In the economy of God there is but one standard by which an individual can succeed—there is but one for a race. This country demands that *every race shall measure itself by the American standard.* . . . During the next half century and more my race must continue passing through the severe American crucible. We are to be tested in our patience, our forbearance, our perseverance, our power to endure wrong . . . to economize, to acquire and use skill; in our ability to compete . . . to be great and yet small, learned and yet simple, high and yet the servant of all. This is the passport to all that is best in the life of our republic, and the Negro must possess it or be debarred.[78] (Italics mine.)

Having affirmed them generously, he went on to secure their support in stigmatizing intolerant whites. "No member of your race in any part of our country can harm the meanest member of mine without the proudest and bluest blood in Massachusetts being degraded."[79] Harlan correctly suggests that Washington allied himself with elite whites against the white masses and even played the two against each other.[80] Clearly, he sought to increase the white elite's sense of responsibility both for the racist behavior of working-class whites and the gradual progress of hardworking blacks.

One of the tragedies of American racism is that Washington felt he had to support a cultural matrix that did not recognize African Americans as possessors of a distinguished history and culture. The more blacks sought to test the melting pot thesis, the more they were reminded that they were unwanted and indissoluble ingredients. For instance, blacks fought in World War I but only in segregated units.

Regrettably, Washington was seduced by the New England cultural ethos, which compromised his appreciation of cultural pluralism. Yet, his views are understandable in light of the ends he sought to achieve. The relative utility of cultural pluralism or monism must be decided by criteria such as the capacity to unify sectional interests, increase the productivity of laborers, and neutralize white racism. He was convinced that a monistic allegiance to a "single standard" could best achieve these ends.

Now I wish to focus on the claims that he pressed in the public realm. In general, we can say that his optimism about America's economic and racial future led him to advance minimal reparations claims for economic justice and educational opportunities.

In a speech titled "The Negro and His Relation to the Economic Progress of the South," he urged whites to remember that they were

> dealing with a people who were forced to come here without their consent and in the face of a most earnest protest. This *gives the Negro a claim* upon your sympathy and generosity that no other race can possess. Besides, though forced from his native land into residence of a country that was not of his choosing, he has *earned his right* to the title of American citizen by obedience to the law, by patriotism and fidelity, and by the millions which his brawny arms have added to the wealth of this country.[81] (Italics mine.)

Later in that speech he argued, "Your duty to the Negro will not be fulfilled till you have made of him that highest type of American citizen, in intelligence, usefulness, and morality."[82] At least two points should be noted here.

First, he believed that duties and obligations create legitimate expectations and rights. Because whites had benefited from the slave labor of Africans, they were obliged to respond to the basic needs of a now free African-American population. If whites had not disrupted African life with the slave trade, Africans would possess no compelling claims on the resources of whites. As a consequence of the incalculable African contribution to the economic stature of America, however, their destinies in the New World became inseparably intertwined. For this reason, Africans could advance legitimate claims in the public sphere rather than relying on the private benevolence of individual whites. He stated, "In the evolution of the South, it seems to me that we have reached that period where private philanthropy and the Christian church of the white South should, in large degree, share directly in the elevation of the Negro."[83] The obligations of white Christians to pay outstanding debts and to assist their less fortunate partners gave rise to legitimate expectations and rights among blacks. In addition to possessing the right to adequate compensation for past suffering and exploitation, blacks legitimately expected to be recognized as American citizens. He believed that whites were obligated to make good on their Christian commitments to the poor until blacks became good citizens. Concomitantly, blacks were obligated to make good on their aspirations to become industrious, patriotic, law-abiding fellow citizens.

Second, Washington measured fair compensation in concrete economic terms. He argued that the South possessed the climate, soil, material wealth, and opportunities for labor that could solve the problem of black self-improvement.[84] In this context, compensation in the form of jobs and greater opportunities for industrial education and economic self-reliance would not be a burden to the white community. As he put it, "Every dollar that goes into the education of the Negro is an interest-bearing dollar."[85] Although he appreciated and secretly encouraged legislative action to rectify the condition of blacks, he was eager to see compensation for enslavement come in tangible rather than symbolic terms.

Galston notes that the claim-generating status of being in need entails lacking "the ensemble of means needed to realize the goods of preservation and development."[86] Preservation goods are the means required for normal physical maturation and activity. Developmental goods are those required for intellectual, moral and emotional development.[87] Claims of desert rest upon "the possession of some quality that places an individual in a preferred position relative to some good."[88] As we have seen, Washington used both modes of presenting public claims for allocable goods. At times he appealed to whites by noting that blacks deserved economic and educational goods because they contributed to the nation's wealth during slavery. At other times he advanced a needs-based case by comparing the levels of living standards and education enjoyed by blacks and whites.

We have examined Washington's understanding of the authentically free person that I have characterized as the adaptive person. Washington illustrates clearly the African-American tradition of conceiving of authentic liberation in two dimensions—personal and social. In pursuit of economic fulfillment, the adaptive person cultivates personal character virtues and a distinctive religious faith designed to equip him for progress in an industrial era. The adaptive person exercises patience in enduring America's slow progress toward its calling as a true democratic republic but is hopeful and optimistic that America can and will achieve this noble end.

Washington's rare gift was an ability to communicate skillfully his social vision to blacks and whites, elites and the masses, and both northern and southern psyches at a complex time of sectional bitterness, racial tension, and rapid economic growth. He was an effective public moralist because he understood the developing American consciousness and grounded his authority in the American Enlightenment and in the biblical covenant traditions that were its chief sources. He viewed the emerging republic as a whole but understood its divergent parts, and he worked for unity, racial cooperation, and the uplift of the disadvantaged. For these reasons, he will be remembered as a voice for the new Negro, the new South, and the new republic.

2

W. E. B. Du Bois
and the Strenuous Person

History is rarely so cooperative with the passing of controversial persons that it hosts two historic events on the same day and thereby confers a transcendent quality on both. On 28 August 1963, the civil rights movement achieved a grand moral victory as a quarter of a million people gathered before the eyes of the nation and the world for the March on Washington. The same day, Dr. William Edward Burghardt Du Bois came to the end of his long life in Accra, Ghana. Du Bois had been an early agitator and organizer of the struggle for black equality but later trod a lonely path into socialism and communism. Although the civil rights movement did not embrace his more radical social strategies, those who gathered at the Lincoln Memorial reverently paused in silence to remember their extraordinary patron saint.

"The doctor," as he was affectionately known, lived for ninety-five years and was active as a scholar, activist, and "master of propaganda" for more than eighty of them.[1] This time span should be remembered when considering the Du Bois corpus because the contours of his social and intellectual worlds evolved during the period. Despite shifts in his political, religious, and social thought, however, one conviction remained constant: the problem of the twentieth century would be the problem of the color line.[2]

Characterizing Du Bois's image of the authentically free person is an intriguing challenge chiefly because his own provocative linguistic style, rich with symbolism and poetry, contains numerous metaphors that aptly summarize his broader moral vision. Nevertheless, after surveying his vast bibliography for a basic image of the authentic person that was operative throughout his career, I decided to use the metaphor of the *strenuous person*. Although Du Bois did not use the phrase himself, I maintain that he was familiar with and adapted elements of this concept, which he learned from William James, his dearest professor and mentor at Harvard University.

+ The Strenuous Person +

In his justly celebrated third book, *The Souls of Black Folk*, and in a speech to the American Negro Academy in 1897, Du Bois characterized the social and existential tension of the American Negro as an "unreconciled striving." As he diagnosed this tension, he maintained that the Negro's attempt to bear two identities—modern American and ancient African—in a society hostile to the latter led to profound frustration and anguish. The central question of his public life seemed to be, How might blacks achieve personal wholeness and societal power without ignoring their cultural indebtedness to Africa, America and Europe? For him, part of the answer lay in destroying the pseudo-intellectual foundations of racism through rigorous and socially transformative scholarship. After delegitimating the myths of black inferiority and of white male supremacy, racial hostility would gradually give way to true cultural pluralism and racial cooperation. Only in this milieu would the Negro experience the possibility of merging a divided identity into a unified self. As he diagnosed the black psyche, he saw a temporarily divided self that could be reconciled; the damage was not permanent. I am convinced that Du Bois's insight into that process of personal and social transformation through reconciliation has much to contribute to contemporary understandings of personal wholeness amid social oppression.

In 1897, during the period of Booker T. Washington's rapid ascendance to national stature, the twenty-nine-year-old Du Bois offered the most penetrating and brilliant psychosocial and political diagnosis of African-American life ever recorded:

> Here, then is the dilemma, and it is a puzzling one, I admit. No
> Negro who has given earnest thought to the situation of his people

in America has failed, at some time in life, to find himself at these crossroads; has failed to ask himself at some time: what, after all, am I? Am I an American or am I a Negro? Can I be both? Or is it my duty to cease to be a Negro as soon as possible and be an American? It is such incessant self-questioning and the hesitation that arises from it, that is making the present period a time of vacillation and contradiction for the American Negro. . . .

Here, it seems to me, is the reading of the riddle that puzzles so many of us. We are Americans, not only by birth and by citizenship, but by our political ideals, our language, our religion. Farther than that, our Americanism does not go. At that point, we are Negroes, members of a vast historic race that from the very dawn of creation has slept, but half awakening in the dark forests of its African fatherland. We are the first fruits of this new nation, the harbinger of that black tomorrow which is yet destined to soften the whiteness of the Teutonic today. We are that people whose subtle sense of song has given America its only American music, its only American fairy tales, its only touch of pathos and humor amid its mad money-getting plutocracy.[3]

Six years later, in a distilled form that is well known to all students of Du Bois, he wrote,

One ever feels his *twoness*—an American, a Negro; two souls, two thoughts, two unreconciled strivings; two warring ideals in one dark body, whose dogged strength alone keeps it from being torn asunder.

The history of the American Negro is the history of this strife,—this longing to attain self-conscious manhood, to merge his double self into a better and truer self.[4] (Italics mine.)

Throughout his thought, Du Bois employed the language of "striving" to characterize the overall mood of the individual's life. In *The Souls of Black Folk*, he reported that the Negro was nearly torn asunder by two "unreconciled strivings."[5] In *Dusk of Dawn*, he suggested that blacks must "live, and eat and strive, and still hold unfaltering commerce with the stars."[6] Before quoting the unalienable rights doctrine of the Declaration of Independence, he claimed, "By every civilized and peaceful method we must strive for the rights which the world accords to men, clinging unwaveringly to those great words which the sons of the Fathers would fain forget: 'We hold these truths to be self-evident.' "[7] Each of these statements and numerous others demonstrate the persistent theme of dialectical tension and conflict in his thought.

For Du Bois, authentically free living transpired amid great tensions, negations, high energies, ambitions, risks, and triumphs, but the strenuous person could not function constantly at such high levels of tension and energy. Therefore, Du Bois prudently postulated a complementary dimension to the conflictual, strenuous mood of the moral life. Flowing from the African spirit of "pathos and humor," it would be a relaxed, disengaged, more pacific, almost mystical moment in human existence.

In an essay wonderfully titled "The Gift of the Spirit," he expanded on this redemptive feature of African spirituality to describe it as a

> peculiar quality which the Negro has injected into American life and civilization. It is hard to define or characterize it—a certain spiritual joyousness; a sensuous, tropical love of life, in vivid contrast to the cool and cautious New England reason; a slow and dreamful conception of the universe, a drawling and slurring of speech, an intense sensitiveness to spiritual values.[8]

In the essay "Black Labor," he alluded to the process by which black workers of the past balanced work and leisure and claimed this ability to be a humanizing virtue that should not be mistaken for laziness.

> The black tropical worker . . . looked upon work as a necessary evil and maintained his right to balance the relative allurements of leisure and satisfaction at any particular day. . . .
>
> The white laborer therefore brought to America the habit of regular, continuous toil which he regarded as a great moral duty. The black laborer brought the idea of toil as a necessary evil ministering to the pleasure of life. While the gift of the white laborer made America rich . . . it will take the psychology of the black man to make it happy.[9]

In contrast to Washington's profound allegiance to the Puritan work ethic, Du Bois counseled against a stoic, hyperactive regimenting of personality and vocation. He anticipated and recommended a proven antidote to the "type A" compulsive personality of modern, industrial culture. Furthermore, because this relaxed dimension was conceived to be a complementary or alternating moment in the ongoing dialectic of strenuous living, Du Bois effectively discouraged people from viewing it as an avenue for escaping obligations to struggle for social change.

Although he was the recipient of a "partially Puritan" upbringing, Du Bois celebrated and affirmed laughter, music, beauty, contemplation, and art as necessary elements of the relaxed mood. Testifying for himself, he claimed to have "tested every normal appetite" and explored the realms of nature, aesthetics, and friendship in search of sensible, enriching pleasures.[10] This led him to characterize his thirteen years of teaching at Atlanta University as years of "hard work and hard play."[11] Through his writings and personal life, he sought to make African-American spirituality widely available in American public life. Indeed, he believed that this source of personal renewal would be critical to human fulfillment in an industrial age.

+ Biographical Sketch +

W. E. Burghardt Du Bois's life was distinguished by an extraordinary education, wide travel, boundless literary and political energies, and an inimitable gift for introspection. Certainly a rare phenomenon in literature, he published three separate autobiographies in which he set forth the salient events of his life against the backdrop of major currents of the time.

In 1920, he published *Darkwater: Voices from Within the Veil*, in which he summarized his thought in the fifth decade of his life. In that work are the many forces that thereafter shaped his thinking: pragmatism, African-American nationalism, Pan-Africanism, the concept of the Third World, socialism, and an evolutionary optimism.[12] In 1940, at the age of seventy, he published his first full-length autobiography, *Dusk of Dawn: An Essay Toward an Autobiography of a Race Concept*. In addition to providing a self-portrait, he defended his position that voluntary self-segregation was the best means of progress for blacks and stressed that he was not a communist and did not believe in the dogma of inevitable revolution in order to correct economic justice.[13] He did affirm adamantly, however, Marx's analysis of the economic foundations of civilization.[14]

In his ninetieth year, 1958, he wrote the draft of his final self-portrait, *The Autobiography of W. E. B. Du Bois: A Soliloquy on Viewing My Life from the Last Decade of Its First Century*. Du Bois considered this volume to be a conventional autobiography in which he claimed "to review my life as frankly and fully as I can."[15] Nevertheless, he used the occasion to articulate his faith in the ultimate, albeit "slow and difficult," triumph of communism as he defined it.[16]

Du Bois was born in Great Barrington, a little town in western Massachusetts, on 23 February 1868. His mother's family, the Burghardts, were among the oldest inhabitants of the valley in which there were approximately twenty-five blacks in a population of five thousand. In 1867 his parents, Alfred Du Bois and Mary Burghardt, married against the wishes of her family, and one year later Alfred moved to New Milford, Connecticut, to establish a home for his family. However, Mary complied with the wishes of her family to remain at home and ignored her husband, who never returned to Great Barrington. As a consequence, Mary sank into depression, and Du Bois never saw his father again. From reports he received, he inferred that his father was "a dreamer—romantic, indolent, kind, unreliable. He had in him the making of a poet, an adventurer."[17]

Du Bois and his mother were cared for by the extended Burghardt family and neighbors until grandfather Othello died. Later, his "worrying mother" had a paralytic stroke that caused lameness in her left leg and a withered left hand. She died after Du Bois's high school graduation in 1884.

The black Burghardts had attended schools for several generations so young William's regular attendance was expected. Early in his educational career, he distinguished himself through intellectual prowess and leadership ability. In *Darkwater*, he recalled his experience as the only black student in his class.

> Very gradually—I cannot now distinguish the steps, though here and there I remember a jump or a jolt—but very gradually I found myself assuming quite placidly that I was different from other children. At first I think I connected the difference with a manifest ability to get my lessons rather better than most and to recite with a certain happy, almost taunting glibness, which brought frowns here and there. Then slowly, I realized that some folks, a few, even several, actually considered my brown skin a misfortune; once or twice I became painfully aware that some human beings even thought it a crime. I was not for a moment daunted—although, of course, there were days of secret tears—rather I was spurred to tireless effort. If they beat me at anything, I was grimly determined to make them sweat for it![18]

In *Dusk of Dawn,* he reported on the behavior of white class-mates who did not seek out his company.

> They were the losers who did not ardently court me and not I, which seemed to be proven by the fact that I had no difficulty in outdoing them in nearly all competition, especially intellectual. In athletics I was not outstanding, I was only moderately good at baseball and football; but at running, exploring, story-telling and planning of intricate games, I was often if not always the leader.[19]

As a teenager he "religiously attended" the town meetings every spring and saw in them the essence of democracy, New England style.[20] He also began to collect a personal library and to write and submit articles for the weekly *New York Globe,* edited by the then-radical black journalist T. Thomas Fortune.[21]

Du Bois recalled that the town had five churches and that he was a proud member of the First Congregational Church. He and his mother were the only black members, but he recalled never having felt discrimination among the leading citizens of the town. Although his family on both sides had been Episcopalians, he and his mother joined the church that was nearer home and contained many acquaintances. Fondly, he remembered Sunday school: "I was quite in my element and led in discussions, with embarrassing questions, and long disquisitions. I learned much of the Hebrew scriptures. I think I must have been both popular and a little dreaded, but I was very happy."[22]

Du Boisian scholar Arnold Rampersad suggests that in that church Du Bois was directly exposed to the fundamental doctrines of New England Puritanism.[23] Although he later scorned organized religion, he retained a lifelong grasp on the rules of Puritan ethics. According to the American philosopher George Santayana, Calvinists oscillate between a profound sense of lowliness and a "paradoxical elation of the spirit."[24] This definition aptly describes Du Bois's basic spiritual and psychic temper. His conscience nurtured a profound sense of duty that often was mistaken to be moral elitism. Although he understood himself to be special, an aristocratic spirit different from others, in later years he was also a champion of the masses and struggled prophetically on their behalf. However, this conscience frequently conflicted with his democratic spirit and enjoyment of the unrestrained "anarchy of the spirit."[25] Somehow he thrived on this tension and channeled his boundless energies into noble and humane causes. By combining the sensuous, joyous qualities of African existence with a Calvinist conscience, he laid hold upon a fascinating way of living morally. In the process, he helped to create and call upon a developing sense of noblesse oblige among elite blacks, an appeal he addressed to the "talented tenth," the educated, professional class.

With the generous help of local church folk, Du Bois attended Fisk University, where he was plunged into a southern, predominantly black culture. He observed and participated in the social refinements of black middle-class life in the South, but also determined to "know something of the Negro in the country districts."[26] He taught summer school in eastern Tennessee and observed firsthand "a region where the world was split into white and black halves."[27] As a college student he began to lose faith in the Congregational theological structure as he observed southern racism with its lynchings and the complicity of the churches. Also during this time, he was exposed to the force of new scientific ideas, especially Herbert Spencer's sociology. Here was born the hope that empirical investigation, the statistical method, and unbiased evaluation might lead people away from racial prejudice toward truth and a better reality. Among his many achievements was that of enlisting new social scientific methods in the struggle for black equality. Indeed, scholarship could possess a socially transformative edge.

After graduating from Fisk, he attended Harvard, where he studied under the eminent philosopher William James. He was a frequent guest at the James household and stated that he "became a devoted follower of James at the time he was developing his pragmatic philosophy."[28] Although Du Bois did not mention the specific influence of James's theory of the tripartite self on his own conception of the Negro's divided self, parallels suggest that Du Bois might have adapted some of his mentor's ideas.[29]

In addition to James's probable influence on Du Bois's conceptions of the divided and unified self, James's reflections on the "strenuous mood" are likely to have resonated deeply with young Du Bois's own temperament and helped to bring into focus his dynamic conception of human fulfillment. Especially intriguing is the parallel between James's description of dual versions of the moral life and

Du Bois's characterization of the complementary, alternating rhythms of African-American life. In his essay "The Moral Philosopher and the Moral Life," James noted that

> the deepest difference, practically, in the moral life of man is the difference between the easy-going and the strenuous mood. When in the easy-going mood the shrinking from present ill is our ruling consideration. The strenuous mood, on the contrary, makes us quite indifferent to present ill, if only the greater ideal be attained.[30]

In his study of James's thought, *Pluralism and Personality*, Don Browning notes,

> In *Varieties of Religious Experience* and his other religious writings, James achieved a synthesis between a mystical and an ethical view of life. His vision of the strenuous life was located firmly within a broader mystical vision of life. His emphasis on responsible individual action on behalf of the wider community was undergirded by an equally strong accent upon the mystical presence of God. . . .
>
> James brings mysticism into the service of the strenuous and ethical life. The mystical experience—that boundary-breaking experience of sensing a deeper unity of relatedness with God and the world—makes a definite contribution to the strenuous life. It gives us a broader sense of relatedness to the whole of life. . . .
>
> For this reason the mystical experience can charge the ethical act with a heightened sense of spontaneity and joy . . . [it] can mitigate the strain stemming from the challenge and effort of the ethical mode of existence.[31]

Although Du Bois did not advocate mystical experience, his vision of the moral life incorporated central elements of African spirituality found in slave religion and the culture of free blacks. We may never know the extent to which the teacher and pupil influenced each other, but clearly with regard to the character of the moral life, both were contributing to the same conversation. From the perspective of this study, Du Bois's contribution was more significant because courageously he introduced into the conversation resources for spiritual renewal from an African-American perspective and thereby asserted the public significance of an otherwise despised people.

With his graduation from Harvard, Du Bois became its first black Ph.D. recipient. Before that milestone, he attended the University of Berlin for two years of study in economics, history, and political science. In 1894, after an exhilarating period of travel and exploration of European culture, he returned to teach classics at Wilberforce College. He arrived with the cane and gloves of his German student days to the amusement of many locals.[32] Once, during a casual visit to the campus chapel where a student meeting was under way, he was invited to offer an extemporaneous prayer. He refused and nearly lost his job. Many did not know what to make of this curious but brilliant young professor. He moved on to the University of Pennsylvania where, as an assistant instructor, he conducted his famous study of urban black life, *The Philadelphia Negro* (1899).[33] There he was able to test his convictions regarding the value of social scientific studies in combating the pseudoscience of racial bigots. As he put it,

> The Negro problem was in my mind a matter of systematic investigation and intelligent understanding. The world was thinking wrong about race, because it did not know. The ultimate evil was stupidity.[34]

In 1897, two years after Booker T. Washington's famous Atlanta Exposition address, Du Bois was hired by President Horace Bumstead of Atlanta University to head the department of sociology. Prior to then, he corresponded with Washington about the possibility of joining the Tuskegee faculty. One can speculate about how African-American history might have been different had Du Bois gone to Tuskegee instead of Atlanta.

During his thirteen years of "hard work and hard play" at Atlanta University, he launched annual sociological studies of black life and helped to organize the Niagara Movement of black intellectual activists, which later became a founding organization of the National Association for the Advancement of Colored People. Most significantly, in 1903 he published *The Souls of Black Folk*, which established his national reputation as an ideological opponent to Washington. In 1910, he became the editor of *The Crisis*, the NAACP's official magazine. Through this news organ Du Bois found his way into households around the nation. For twenty years he interpreted to the world the "hindrances and aspirations of American Negroes."[35]

In subsequent years he wrote novels, joined and resigned from the Socialist Party, organized the Pan-African Congress, and in 1934

returned to Atlanta University after the NAACP accepted his res-
ignation amid controversy. Ten years later he retired and returned
to New York in order to support anticolonialist movements and the
spread of international socialism. In 1950, he became a candidate
for the U.S. Senate on the American Labor Party ticket. A year
later, following the death of his first wife, Nina Gomer Du Bois, he
married Shirley Graham, an intellectual, activist, and daughter of
a Methodist minister. He began a period of controversial international travels to China (1959) and the Soviet Union (a three-month
stay), which culminated in his joining the American Communist
Party. At the age of ninety-three, Du Bois accepted Kwame Nkru-
mah's invitation and returned to Ghana, where he planned a mul-
tivolume *Encyclopedia Africana*. As Malcolm X and Martin Luther
King, Jr., were becoming the foremost voices of black activism in
America, Du Bois became a citizen of Ghana (February 1963), where
he died in August 1963.

Before his departure for Ghana in 1961, he entrusted to the
historian Herbert Aptheker a large collection of letters and papers
in which an envelope of prayers was discovered. In 1980, Aptheker
published the small collection which Du Bois had written in pencil
between early 1909 and the spring of 1910 *(Prayers for Dark People)*.
Aptheker's introduction calls attention to numerous little-known facts
about Du Bois's religiosity, such as his familiarity with biblical literature (which is illustrated in the prayers), his affection for talking
to children, his abstinence from hard liquor, his high valuation of
courtesy, promptness, sartorial care, rigid frugality, and honesty,
and his dislike for denominational Christianity, which grew out of
his conviction that the churches had ignored the revolutionary character of the teachings of Jesus, for which he maintained high admiration.[36]

Despite Du Bois's impatience with Christianity, Aptheker suggests,

> Personally . . . Du Bois never lost a certain sense of religiosity,
> of some possible super-natural creative force. In many respects,
> Du Bois's religious outlook in his last two or three decades might
> be classified as agnostic, but certainly not atheistic, this remained
> true even when he chose to join the Communist party.[37]

Rampersad goes further than Aptheker by suggesting of Du
Bois's religion, "Now agnostic, now atheistic, Du Bois wandered

between Matthew Arnold's Hellenism and Hebraism, but he ended by adding to the Puritan God of his youth the deified ideals of Greek intellectualism. The instability of his religion does not deny its vitality or its scope. The purpose of life was aspiration to the ideal."[38]

In the end, Du Bois was a complex and somewhat lonesome figure animated by paradoxical if not polar forces: strict Puritan ethics and a joyous indulgence in the "anarchy of the spirit"; a profound sense of obligation to the masses and a natural identification with the black elite; black nationalism and communist-inspired visions of a world community. Among the less-emphasized elements of his legacy is his dynamic image of the authentically free life.

+ Conception of Human Fulfillment +

We now turn to Du Bois's substantive reflections on the moral life. I have organized these reflections into four categories that were persistent concerns throughout his life: civic virtue, economic empowerment, personal refinement, and rational religion. Although he tended to emphasize the importance of political goods for an authentically free life (voting, office holding, etc.), after the collapse of Wall Street, he attributed greater significance to economic goods. This shift represented an expansion of his moral vision, which included an endorsement of some Washingtonian ideas, such as voluntary self-segregation and industrial education.

Civic Virtue

Du Bois believed that full political participation, especially voting and office holding, was essential for personal fulfillment and social justice. Recall that his model of public life was the New England town meeting where, as a boy, he had listened with rapt attention to the vigorous but civil debates that preceded voting. He considered voting to be the elemental demonstration of civic virtue. Informed voting was the result of a process in which each citizen reached defensible conclusions after being persuaded by the better candidate's argument and platform. Through significant participation in civic life, blacks, along with other Americans, would become virtuous citizens and the republic would become just.

Du Bois clashed forcefully with Washington in regard to the necessity of voting for an authentically free life. For Washington, economic self-reliance was the irreplaceable foundation of black power and self-esteem. Blacks' contribution to America should be measureable in monetary terms. Although Du Bois affirmed this strategy as a feature of authentic liberation, during his presocialist years he consistently asserted the priority of the political. He stated that "Negroes must insist continually, in season and out of season, that voting is necessary to modern manhood."[39] Washington sought to bracket the controversial subject of black enfranchisement while fostering cooperation between blacks and whites around common economic interests. Du Bois could not ignore the self-evident and inclusive claims concerning human equality found in the Declaration of Independence, the Constitution with its Thirteenth, Fourteenth, and Fifteenth Amendments, and the Bible. Citizenship and equality before God and the law were not negotiable. Du Bois felt that blacks should be impatient about demanding justice from a nation founded on tenets contained in these sacred texts. Through relentless struggle, the distant utopia of black citizenship could become a living reality.

For Du Bois, the value of voting could extend beyond the expression of personal political preferences. From a defensive perspective, voting was a means of securing political liberties for the group and of preventing subtle forms of reenslavement. As he put it, "The power of the ballot we need in sheer self-defence—else what shall save us from a second slavery?"[40] From a proactive perspective, political behavior could be a form of moral action by which blacks, especially the talented tenth, could project their understanding of public righteousness and interracial cooperation. In *The Souls of Black Folk*, he argued,

> We are awakening to the fact that the perpetuity of republican institutions on this continent depends on the purification of the ballot, the civic training of voters, and raising voting to the level of a solemn duty which a patriotic citizen neglects to his peril and to the peril of his children's children—in this day, when we are *striving for a renaissance of civic virtue,* what are we going to say to the black voter of the South? Are we going to tell him still that politics is a disreputable and useless form of human activity? Are we going to induce the best class of Negroes to take less and less interest in government, and to give up their right to take such an interest, without a protest?[41] (Italics mine.)

Conscious of the continuing sectional strife engendered by the Civil War and Reconstruction, Du Bois urged whites to allow blacks to participate fully in the "renaissance of civic virtue," in which all Americans possessed a stake. Marching into the twentieth century, America was a new nation requiring a rebirth of civic virtue and vision. Wise leaders understood the fragility of the new nation's identity. This perspective explains Du Bois's assertion that the perpetuity of the republic itself—rather than a particular group's social position—depended on raising voting to the level of a solemn duty. Such duties compelled forward-looking, virtuous citizens to act on behalf of the common good of the present society and of their children as well. Moreover, Du Bois insisted that room be made in the public arena for elite blacks to contribute their vision of a just America.

In a speech delivered to the Interracial Conference in Washington, D.C., on 19 December 1928 ("The Negro Citizen"), he argued that "when democracy fails for one group in the United States, it fails for the nation; and when it fails for the United States it fails for the world."[42] Here he linked the status of the nation's moral health to that of its disadvantaged and disfranchised members. He continued:

> In the past we have deplored disfranchisement in the South because of its effect on the Negro. But it is not simply that the Negro remains a slave as long as he is disfranchised, but that southern white laborers are dragged inevitably down to the Negro's position, and that the decent white South is not only deprived of decent government, but of all real voice in both local and national government. It is as true today as it ever was that the nation cannot exist half slave and half free.[43]

As he pointed out the discrepancies between America's democratic rhetoric and her discriminatory reality, he appealed to a sense of civic virtue presumed to exist in the wider body politic. He challenged the government and every citizen to demonstrate moral courage and integrity by granting and protecting the citizenship rights of blacks. If Americans possessed civic virtues such as tolerance for people who are different, courage to act in public upon what is right, and the integrity to be honest about one's misdeeds toward others, then they would recognize the immorality and irrationality of a nation seeking to be half slave and half free. In his rationally forceful style, he reaffirmed the interconnectedness of all citizens in a democracy and argued that the freedom and potential for ful-fillment of whites was compromised by the presence of their dis-franchised black fellow citizens.

Whereas Washington appealed to whites' sense of self-interest in order to elicit their benevolence, Du Bois appealed to the nobler but more fragile sense of civic virtue and rationality. Washington understood people to be basically selfish; Du Bois understood them to be creatures who aspire toward—and occasionally achieve—moral goodness and virtue.

In the essay "The Emancipation of Democracy," he elaborated the seminal contribution of blacks to the concept and reality of democracy in the West. Also, he demonstrated that even before they had attained citizenship, blacks had exhibited noteworthy civic virtue. To convey the cogency of his argument, I provide the quotation in its entirety.

> Without the help of black soldiers, the independence of the United States could not have been gained in the eighteenth century. But the Negro's contribution to America was at once more subtle and important than these things. Dramatically *the Negro is the central thread of American history.* The whole story turns on him whether we think of the dark and flying slave ship in the sixteenth century, the expanding plantations of the seventeenth, the swelling commerce of the eighteenth, or the fight for freedom in the nineteenth. It was the *black man that raised a vision of democracy in America* such as neither Americans nor Europeans conceived in the eighteenth century and such as they have not even accepted in the twentieth; and yet a conception which *every clear sighted man knows is true and inevitable.*[44] (Italics mine.)
>
> This great vision of the black man was, of course, at first the vision of the few, as visions always are, but it was always there; it grew continuously and it developed quickly from wish to active determination. . . . The democracy established in America in the eighteenth century was not, and was not designed to be, a democracy of the masses of men and it was thus singularly easy for people to fail to see *the incongruity of democracy and slavery.* It was the Negro himself who forced the consideration of this incongruity, who made emancipation inevitable and made the modern world at least consider if not wholly accept the *idea of a democracy including men of all races and colors.*[45] (Italics mine.)

Given the significant role played by blacks in the formation of the American republic, he believed that they were entitled not only to the allocable political goods of citizenship and voting but also to special honor and public recognition as heroes of a sort; that is, by virtue of exceptional behavior, blacks had redeemed America from a schizoid, immoral destiny. As this history became widely known, it might dispel some of the ignorance and misinformation concerning African contributions to America's political traditions. This information might also bring greater dishonor and shame to those who violated the rights of heroic Americans. Du Bois wrote a thick volume on the Reconstruction in which he documented the fact that blacks were not only visionaries of an inclusive democracy but, for those fleeting years, were also competent practitioners thereof. Indeed, the tradition of civic virtue in black history alongside the traditions he observed as a youth ultimately drove him to venture beyond voting to run for the U.S. Senate himself.

Economic Empowerment

Du Bois's faith in political goods and activism remained constant throughout his life, but he also accorded major, even coequal importance to economic goods following the collapse of Wall Street in 1929. During this period he also ventured further into the company of socialists as he searched for a systemic alternative to capitalism. At the same time he denied vehemently that he was a communist. Substantively, his vision of the strenuous life expanded to valorize manual labor and industrial education.

In *Dusk of Dawn,* he admitted that he had been slow to recognize the importance of economics. "It was not until I was long out of college and had finished the first phase of my teaching career that I began to see clearly the connection between economics and politics; the fundamental influence of man's efforts to earn a living upon all his other efforts."[46] He observed, "I began to unite my economics and politics; but I still assumed that . . . the political realm was dominant."[47] Following the crash of 1929, he consistently stated that black advancement in an unrestrained capitalistic economy was futile. Throughout the pages of *Crisis,* he reported that the crash revealed "the fundamental weakness of our system" and affirmed the necessity of Marxian-inspired principles and practices of economic cooperation. He also embraced Washington's views concerning the need for voluntary self-segregation and self-reliance in the interest of developing collective black power.

In his speech, "A Negro Nation Within a Nation," delivered in 1935, he claimed, "The main weakness of the Negro's position is that since emancipation he has never had an adequate economic foundation."[48] He commended Washington's effort to provide a "comprehensive economic plan" that sought to incorporate blacks into white industries. He also observed, in contrast, that Washington did not foresee twentieth-century developments such as the concentration of industries, land monopoly, and the mechanization of the workplace.[49]

Du Bois urged young blacks to create alliances with and prove their utility to the labor movement and to demonstrate their efficiency as workers, managers, and controllers of capital.[50] He called for a united college and vocational system, greater emphasis on engineering and industrial planning, and a dedication to the ideals of poverty, work, knowledge, and sacrifice.[51] While affirming the proper role of each vocation in the black community, he sketched his vision of how black professionals and black laborers could cooperate in the service of economic and political liberation.

> There exists a chance for the Negroes to organize a cooperative state within their own group. By letting Negro farmers feed Negro artisans, and Negro technicians guide Negro home industries, and Negro thinkers plan this integration of cooperation, while Negro artists dramatize and beautify the struggle, economic independence can be achieved.[52]

He also maintained,

> With the use of their political power, their power as consumers, and their brainpower . . . Negroes can develop in the United States an economic nation within a nation, able to work through inner cooperation, to found its own institutions, to educate its genius, and at the same time, without mob violence or extremes of race hatred, to keep in helpful touch and cooperate with the mass of the nation.[53]

His ideas regarding a "cooperative state" within the black community and of a "nation within a nation" are intriguing and provocative. Going beyond Washington's emphasis on the power inherent in economic goods (income, property, self-employment), Du Bois saw an even greater mobilization of the black community's latent power emerging from the concerted deployment of political goods (voting, office holding), economic goods, and high scholastic performance ("brainpower"). With regard to the fundamental conviction that the resources for personal and group uplift reside already in the black community, both moralists were allied.

Rampersad commends Du Bois's program as an "innovative response to circumstances peculiar to the Depression as well as to factors constant in the modern history of race relations in the United States."[54] So understood, we might conclude that Du Bois's advocacy of voluntary self-segregation and limited cooperation with whites was situationally rational. It was certainly that, but it was more as well. As he continued to read and travel, Du Bois seemed to apprehend truths about America and the West that Washington had come to know by virtue or fault of his southern heritage; that is, Du Bois came to see the deep and seemingly permanent nature of white racism and the social evils that emerge when capitalism operates unregulated. Instead of adapting creatively and redemptively to these realities as Washington suggested, however, Du Bois's faith in the black community's self-rehabilitating potential deepened, and he continued to propagandize strenuously for Pan-Africanism and international socialism.

Personal Refinement

Du Bois's view of personal development was impressively diversified and comprehensive. He claimed, "Life is . . . (1) Beauty and health of body; (2) Mental clearness and creative genius; (3) Spiritual goodness and receptivity; (4) Social adaptability and constructiveness."[55] This image reminds us of his familiarity with classical Greek culture and thought; he had taught classics at Wilberforce. Indeed, the quest for human perfectibility was a prominent motif in much Greek thought.

In a commencement address at Fisk University in 1938, Du Bois expanded on this outline while responding to the questions, What is life? What is it for? and What is its great end? He replied,

> Life is the fullest, most complete enjoyment of the possibilities of human existence. It is the development and broadening of the feelings and emotions, through sound and color, line and form. It is technical mastery of the media that these paths and emotions need for expression of their full meaning. It is the free enjoyment of every normal appetite. It is giving rein to the creative impulse,

in thought and imagination. Here roots the rise of the Joy of Living, of music, painting, drawing, sculpture and building, hence rise literature with romance, poetry and essay, hence rise Love, Friendship, emulation, and ambition, and the ever widening realms of thought in increasing circles of apprehended and interpreted Truth.[56]

He believed that this experience of fulfillment was available to people who were "sufficiently well-bred to make human contact bearable, if they learned to read and write and reason; if they [had] character enough to distinguish between right and wrong and strength enough to do right; if they [could] earn a decent living and know the world in which they live."[57] As he spoke these words to an assemblage of black college graduates, he sought to inspire them to go beyond merely making a good living measured in material terms. Du Bois invited these new members of the black elite to live strenuously, to exhibit an intense, unrestrained joie de vivre. Du Bois sought to push them out into a world of possibility with a sense of confidence and mastery that would empower them to overcome hindrances to their fullest and "most complete enjoyment of the possibilities of human existence."

Although his vision of personal development was richly diversified, he consistently asserted the fundamental importance of intellectual development through formal education. Because intellectual development occupied a privileged position in Du Bois's thought, education became the principal allocable good for which he advanced claims based on obvious need and desert. In the essay "The Freedom to Learn," he asserted that "of all the civil rights for which the world has struggled . . . the right to learn is undoubtedly the most fundamental."[58]

During an earlier commencement address at Fisk (1898), he asserted,

> [College provides] a glimpse of the higher life, the broader possibilities of humanity, which is granted to the man who, amid the rush and roar of living, pauses four short years to learn what living means.
>
> The vision of the rich meaning of life, which comes to you as students, as men of culture, comes dimly or not at all to the plodding masses of men, and even to men of high estate it comes too often blurred and distorted by selfishness and greed. But you have seen it in the freshness and sunshine of youth: here you have talked with Aristotle and Shakespeare.[59]

Again, his elite, classical cultural bias is obvious as he acknowledges that for the most part the masses of blacks and whites do not, without the aid of formal education, grasp the breadth of the higher life or fully participate in its vast enjoyments. For Du Bois, the ideal education entailed schooling in the liberal arts, including heavy doses of the sciences, the classics, and practical applications to uplifting the disadvantaged. We should underscore the importance of this redemptive social dimension of an authentic education. For Du Bois, a gifted individual was not "free" to pursue personal fulfillment while ignoring the plight of his or her oppressed kin. The talented tenth were to be missionaries of learning and culture. As he put it, "The German works for Germany, the Englishman serves England, and it is *the duty of the Negro to serve his blood and lineage,* and so working, each for each, and all for each, we realize the goal of each for all."[60] (Italics mine.)

Personally, he did not receive such an ennobling, authentic education in any single university. While at Fisk he came to know African-American culture and religion and the horrific oppression of southern blacks. Following the turn of the century, while waves of southern blacks fled north in search of better opportunities, Du Bois was traveling in the opposite direction with the same end in view. Indeed, his journey from the north to the south became the prototype for subsequent generations of young blacks who made the mythic pilgrimage to the South, particularly to attend black colleges, as a way of discovering, refining and celebrating their African-American identities. At Harvard he embraced and appropriated the highest expressions of New England American life and thought. In Berlin he came to acknowledge America's indebtedness to Europe and the wider world. Hence, attaining an authentic education would require nothing less than strenuous intentionality, pursuit, and seriousness. The reward, however, would be worth the struggle.

Pursuant to making recommendations to improve the standard of black education, he diagnosed the state of black higher education at the time.

We hear much of higher Negro education, and yet all people know that there does not exist today in the center of the Negro population a single first-class fully equipped institution, devoted to the higher education of Negroes; not more than three Negro institutions in the South deserves the name of "college" at all. Without doubt the first effective step toward the solving of the Negro question will be the endowment of a Negro college which is not merely a teaching body, but a center of sociological research, in close connection and cooperation with Harvard, Columbia.[61]

Atlanta University, where he spent many years, came closest to his ideal—a research institution committed to the social scientific examination of every aspect of black life and culture.

Rational Religion

We now consider Du Bois's assessment of religious faith in the moral life. As a historian and social scientist, he viewed the vestiges of slave religion within contemporary black religion to be anachronistic and largely dysfunctional in a new industrial age. His ideal of black religion combined the stern moral seriousness of Puritanism with the gifts of African spirituality. He did not wish to deny blacks the joyful, sensuous, energizing experience of the sacred; rather, he sought to put those resources in the service of the great struggle for racial and economic justice. Consequently, his rhetorical strategy varied depending upon the intended audience. When among preachers, he gently endorsed the nonmystical, morally serious religious life. When speaking to laypersons like himself, he heaped scorn upon irresponsible and visionless clergy and urged the masses to hold them accountable.

Du Bois was fascinated by southern black religion as he observed it in rural Tennessee. While praising much about it, he could not bring himself to become a participant in the "high voltage" worship of black grassroots folk. Recall his experience of dislocation when he first saw a tent revival.

> It was out in the country, far from home, far from my foster home, on a dark Sunday night. The road wandered from our rambling longhouse up the stony bed of a creek . . . until we could hear dimly across the fields a rhythmic cadence of song—soft, thrilling, powerful, that swelled and died sorrowfully in our ears. I was a country school teacher then, fresh from the East, and had never seen a Southern Negro revival. . . . A sort of suppressed terror hung in the air and seemed to seize us—a pythian madness, a demonic possession, that lent a terrible reality to song and word.[62]

Following this account, he discussed the historical importance and distinctiveness of the black preacher, black church music, and the "frenzy" or shout. His phenomenological accounts quickly gave way to social, scientific, and historical analytic commentary, always reminding the reader that he was more the observer than an immediate participant.

Notwithstanding his ambivalent personal posture vis-à-vis traditional black church life, he was acquainted well enough with the essence of African piety to render the following diagnosis of black religion in the crucible of white racism.

> Such a double life, with double thoughts, double duties, and double social classes, must give rise to double words and double ideals, and tempt the mind to pretense or revolt, to hypocrisy or radicalism.
>
> In some such doubtful words and phrases can one perhaps most clearly picture the peculiar ethical paradox that faces the Negro of today and is tingeing [*sic*] and changing his religious life. Feeling that his . . . rights and his dearest ideals are being trampled upon, that the public conscience is ever more deaf to his righteous appeal, and that all the reactionary forces of prejudice, greed, and revenge are daily gaining new strength and fresh allies, the Negro faces no enviable dilemma. Conscious of his impotence, and pessimistic, he often becomes bitter and vindictive and *his religion, instead of a worship, is a complaint and a curse, a wail rather than a hope, a sneer rather than a faith.* On the other hand, another type of mind, shrewder and keener and more tortuous too, sees in the very strength of the anti-Negro movement its patent weaknesses, and with Jesuitic casuistry is deterred by no ethical considerations in the endeavor to turn this weakness to the black man's strength.[63] (Italics mine.)

Based on his observations of blacks in the North and South, he noted the manner in which racism was distorting the forms and emphases of black religion by either reducing it to a passive, plaintive exercise in lamentation or driving it toward militant, nihilistic, potentially explosive activism. He believed that these "two great and hardly reconcilable streams of thought and ethical strivings" lead inevitably either to hypocrisy or anarchy, to compromise or radicalism.[64] However, although these tensions were present throughout the black religious community, most blacks had not yet adopted either ethical extreme. Indeed, he was hopeful that ultimately a new religious awakening would come in America and manifest itself in a racially just society.

Like Washington, Du Bois found the otherworldly, mythic elements in black faith to be expendable. Had they been more intentional methodologically, we could say that both moralists viewed the moral life from the perspective of an ethics of virtue. They believed that the moral life should contain certain identifiable traits of character that manifest themselves in right behavior.

Among the many virtues he sought to embody and inculcate in the talented tenth was self-sacrifice. Without it, they would not be able to serve the community effectively. In 1930 at a commencement address to Howard University, he made his case before the black elite once again.

> When I say sacrifice, I mean sacrifice. I mean a real and definite surrender of personal ease and satisfaction. I embellish it with *no theological fairy tales of a rewarding God or a milk and honey heaven.* I am not trying to scare you into the duty of sacrifice by the fires of a mythical Hell.
>
> To increase abiding satisfaction for the mass of our people, and for all people, someone must sacrifice something of his own happiness. This is a duty only to those who recognize it as a duty. It is silly to tell intelligent human beings: Be good and you will be happy. The truth is today, be good, be decent, be honorable and self-sacrificing and you will not always be happy. You will often be desperately unhappy. You may even be crucified, dead, and buried, and the third day you will be just as dead as the first. But with the death of your happiness may easily come increased happiness and satisfaction and fulfillment for other people—strangers, unborn babes, uncreated worlds. If this is not sufficient incentive, never try it—remain hogs.[65] (Italics mine.)

By 1930, his tolerance for nonverifiable religious truth claims had evaporated entirely. If he could have his way, no doubt he would have surgically removed the supernaturalism from the heart of black religion and grafted onto the tradition a greater emphasis on moral virtues and civic responsibility. Note that Du Bois urged blacks to make sacrifices for the fulfillment of other people, including strangers and unborn generations. For him, authentic Christianity entailed making sacrifices for noble causes such as helping the disadvantaged and creating a just social order.

In order to illustrate how such an ethics of virtue could shape personal piety, I turn to one of his Christmas prayers contained in the collection *Prayers for Dark People.*

> O Thou Incarnate Word of God to man, make us this Christmas night to realize Thy truth: we are not Christians because we profess Thy name and celebrate the ceremonies and idly reiterate the prayers of the church, but only in so far as we really *comprehend and follow the Christ spirit*—we must be poor and not rich, meek and not proud, merciful and not oppressors, peaceful and not warlike or quarrelsome. For the sake of the righteousness of our cause we must bow to persecution and reviling, and again and again turn the stricken cheek to the striker; and above all the cause of our neighbor must be to us dearer than our own cause. This is Christianity. God help us all to be Christians. Amen (Luke 2:8–18).[66] (Italics mine.)

Exhibiting the savvy of a seasoned pastor, in this prayer Du Bois conveys his theological and ethical agenda to the listeners while addressing the deity. Although this discourse assumed the form of a prayer, clearly he was moralizing *in public* about authentic Christian character. He urged the student congregation to comprehend the essence of Christianity by appropriating, cognitively and behaviorally, the virtues and spirit of Jesus Christ.

Whereas Washington's effort to crusade in behalf of such a practical faith led him to establish Phelps Bible Training School, which would directly impact the clergy, Du Bois never institutionalized his concern with rehabilitating black folk religion. Instead, he sought to evangelize through speech making to the black elite and publishing in the literary organ of the NAACP, *The Crisis*. For instance, in his commencement speech at Fisk in 1898 (a decade after his own graduation and eight years after Washington's controversial commencement address in which he lashed black preachers), he stated his case for a learned and liberating clergy, the religious segment of his talented tenth.

> What we need is not more but fewer ministers, but in that lesser number we certainly need earnest, broad, and cultured men; men who do a good deal more than they say; men of broad plans and far-seeing thought; men who will extend the charitable and rescue work of the churches, encourage home-getting, guard the children of the flock, not on Sundays, but on weekdays, make the people use savings banks, and in fine, men who will really be *active agents of social and moral reform* in their communities. There and there only, is the soil which will *transform the mysticism of Negro religion into the righteousness of Christianity.*[67] (Italics mine.)

Again we find evidence of Du Bois's profound respect for the ideals of Christianity, especially sacrifice, poverty, communalism, hard work, and justice. His scorn of institutional Christianity was correctly directed toward churches and ministers who bore little resemblance to the revolutionary Christ spirit. He was especially scathing on the topic of ministers who were not serious about undertaking social and moral uplift in the black community. He argued that

> moreover, the severest charge that can be brought against the Christian education of the Negro in the South during the last thirty years is the reckless way in which sap-headed young fellows, without ability, and in some cases without character have been urged and pushed into the ministry. It is time now to halt. It is time to say to young men like you: qualifications that would be of no service elsewhere are not needed in the church; a general desire to be good, joined to a glib tongue, is not the sort of combination that is going to make the Negro people stop stealing and committing adultery. And, instead of aimless, wholesale invitations to enter this calling of life, we need to put our hands kindly on the shoulders of some young candidates, and tell them firmly that they are not fitted to be heads of the church of Christ.[68]

When ministers and churches were faithful to high ethical ideals, however, he acknowledged their importance for the future of the community. As he put it, "But to those consecrated men who can and will place themselves today at the head of Negro religious life and guide this wavering people to a Christianity pure and holy and true—to those men in the day of reckoning shall surely come the benediction of a useful life, and the 'Well done!' of the Master."[69]

In addition to recognizing the moral and educative function of the black church, he noted that it was the organizational base for any significant mass movement, whether political, economic, or cultural. Du Bois also commended the degree of organizational sophistication in black churches, noting that churches such as Bethel A.M.E. of Philadelphia with its thousands of members "are really governments of men."[70] He also called attention to the reciprocal influence between black and white Christians and observed that the "Methodists and Baptists of America owe much of their condition to the silent but potent influence of their millions of Negro converts."[71]

The Jamaican moralist Marcus Garvey knew better than anyone else of the period how to use the church as an organizational base in the service of political empowerment and instilling race pride. Because Washington, Du Bois, and Garvey were not clergymen, however, the vast majority of church-going blacks were not mobilized in the struggle until the coming of the civil rights movement, the Southern Christian Leadership Conference, and the ministry of Dr. Martin Luther King, Jr.

Given its organizational and motivational power, Du Bois could not ignore or bypass the black church, a lesson worthy of note for contemporary black elites. Given his personal history and evolving identity, he could not become a participant in it. Therefore, he evangelized vigorously among college graduates to expand the ranks of the talented tenth clergy who were capable of leading the churches and the community. They would take the lead in helping the community to develop the ethical virtues necessary for liberation, and they could do this without an excessive reliance upon the supernatural and fantastic elements of slave religion. In his extraordinary prayers and speeches, we find the outline of Du Bois's social gospel.

+ The Just Society +

In this final section, I briefly sketch a Du Boisian vision of the just society. His concern for liberty, individual rights, and distributive justice places him in conversation with numerous liberal moral philosophers. I believe that the benefit of his insights can be expanded by being placed in a broader, coherent philosophical system such as the one developed by John Rawls. Also, the formalism of Rawls's system can be overcome by immersion in mutually critical dialogue with the historical experience of America's most unique minority. As noted in the last chapter, Washington contributes to this dialogue his experience of slavery and evolution toward freedom. From a substantive point of view, this contribution expands the empirical and American historical data base from which moral philosophers should generate theories of justice. No theory of American public life can be adequate without sustained attention to the present implications of the enslavement of Africans or the systematic exclusion of women. Du Bois has much to offer both substantively and methodologically to this conversation.

Du Bois's conception of the just society cohered around two fundamental elements—faith in the democratic republic and a commitment to welfare state, socialist economic principles. He thought the former to be the best guarantor of individual liberty and developmental fulfillment; he saw the latter as a remedy to the exploitative human relations inherent in monopoly capitalism.

If my interpretation is on target, Du Bois's position seems to afffirm the values inherent in Rawls's two principles (extensive individual liberties and affirmative social provisions for the least advantaged) without concurring with his insistence on their serial arrangement.[72] Du Bois vacillated on the relative importance of political and economic goods and allowed for a possible trade-off between the two substantive agendas.

Regarding the democratic republic, he said in 1920:

> The real argument for democracy is, then, that in the people we have the source of that endless life and unbounded wisdom which the rulers of men must have. A given people today may not be intelligent, but through a democratic government that recognizes, not only the worth of the individual to himself, but the *worth of his feelings and experiences to all,* they can educate, not only the individual unit, but generation after generation, until they accumulate vast stores of wisdom. *Democracy alone is the method of showing the whole experience of the race for the benefit of the future* and if democracy tries to exclude women or Negroes or the poor or any class because of innate characteristics which do not interfere with intelligence, then that democracy cripples itself and belies its name.[73] (Italics mine.)

He believed true democracy to be the best system for protecting individual liberties and cultivating the self-governing faculties of individuals and communities. As noted before, this faith was rooted in his early life experience in New England town meetings, where common folk debated matters of public interest.

In 1936, he affirmed the American democratic experiment as a noble effort to validate the common person as a human being possessing inviolable dignity and abilities.

> The meaning of America is the possibilities of the common man. It is a refutation of that widespread assumption that the real makers of the world must always be a small group of exceptional men, while most men are incapable of assisting civilization or achieving culture. The United States proves, if it proves anything, that the

number of men who may by educated and may achieve is much
larger than the world has hitherto assumed.[74]

In such statements, Du Bois demonstrated his profound historical understanding and appreciation for the significance of the
American experiment. Despite the society's fundamental flaws, he
acknowledged the bold, humanistic vision of the dignity of common
individuals that underlay American society. In the republic, the
authentic life could be achieved because individual liberties were
protected from state encroachment and the unfair exercise of liberty
by other citizens. The strenuous person experienced liberation, in
part, by virtue of her or his freedom to toil vigorously for the common
good and his or her own individual fulfillment. The strenuous person,
now a unified self, could also enjoy both (or all) of her or his identities
in a pluralistic culture, as all people and ethnic traditions were
equally respected. However, complete liberation in the democratic
republic was unattainable and compromised by its interrelation with
materialistic, hyperindividualistic monopoly capitalism. Because the
beauty of political democracy and its egalitarian ethos were compromised by gross inequities in the economic system, Du Bois embraced the basic tenets of socialism and welfare statism as a corrective
to America's economic injustices. This brings us to the second fundamental element of his social vision, namely, the socialist or welfare
state.

In his 1958 essay titled, "The Negro and Socialism," he argued
that underneath the historical struggles and growth of world socialism "lay the central idea that men must work for a living, but
that the results of their work must not mainly be to support privileged
persons and concentrate power in the hands of the owners of wealth;
that *the welfare of the mass of people should be the main object of
government.*"[75] (Italics mine.)

He concluded the piece by outlining a platform for blacks.

> Thus it is clear today that the salvation of American Negroes lies
> in socialism. They should *support all measures and men who favor
> the welfare state;* they should vote for government ownership of
> l in industry; they should favor strict regulation of corpo-
> s or their public ownership; they should vote to prevent
> oly from controlling the press and the publishing of opin-
> hey should favor public ownership and control of water,
> , and atomic power; they should stand for a clean ballot,

the encouragement of third parties, independent candidates, and the elimination of graft and gambling on television and even in churches.[76] (Italics mine.)

For Du Bois, the humanistic features of some socialist visions (e.g. preferential care for the poor) possessed greater moral legitimacy and congruence with democracy than did capitalism and other systems designed to reward self-aggrandizement. He urged blacks to realize that "no system of reform offers the American Negro such real emancipation as socialism."[77] Observing the international spread of socialism throughout Africa and Asia, he felt its popularity would inevitably influence American blacks.[78] Thus, he thought authentic freedom to be dependent upon political liberty along with the fair distribution of economic goods and government ownership of capital and industry.

Du Bois's acceptance of the socialist economic agenda was somewhat naive insofar as he did not seem to recognize that individual liberties might be encroached upon by the directive state and that the political achievement of the first principle of justice might thereby by compromised. Moreover, his later vacillation regarding the priority of political over economic goods and concerns makes problematic the assertion that his principal concern was consistently political, and that, like Rawls, he would not have allowed basic liberties to be curtailed in the interest of increasing economic advantages. The vacillation in Du Bois's position could be resolved by recasting his social vision in light of the Rawlsian insistence on the priority of political goods over social and economic ones. Then, however, it would cease to be Du Bois's position. Indeed, part of the wisdom of his pragmatic political philosophy lay precisely in cultivating the proper amount of ambiguity in regard to stating a categorical preference when faced with competing ethical ideals. He seemed to feel that the answer to some questions should be deliberately partial and tentative, awaiting additional information and test results.

Rawls, too, benefits from a dialogue with Du Bois. Du Bois can redeem Rawls's excessively formalistic and idealistic system by providing historically verifiable explanations of the manner in which least-advantaged persons actually perceive themselves in the unjust social structure and of how they develop distorted views of themselves and social reality (false consciousness). Both Rawls and Galston need a Du Boisian explication of the *premoral* struggle for authentic selfhood in order to communicate effectively with large numbers of least-advantaged citizens. The persons about whom Du Bois wrote probably could not find their historical experience represented in contemporary moral philosophy. Their discussions often seem to beg the question of the presence of a coherent, functional self. Du Bois would remind these moral philosophers of the social-psychological prerequisites to moral agency (self-conscious personhood) and that people must become *agents* before they can become *moral agents.* Thus, by virtue of his brilliant analysis of the divided self of black Americans, Du Bois points out significant areas of morally relevant deliberation that most white American moral philosophers fail to engage. If these theoreticians would read the books of people like Du Bois and take them seriously as dialogue partners, then the value and harmonizing potential of philosophy in a pluralistic context might be clearly established. Until that time, we wait expectantly for a truly public philosophy.

An earlier section explains the strategy of discourse Du Bois employed when advancing claims for allocable goods and his notion of civic virtue. By way of summary, we could say that Du Bois employed the rhetoric of desert when addressing the wider public in behalf of oppressed blacks and the rhetoric of need when speaking to the black elite and urging them to help liberate their needy kin.

As we have seen, he vigorously reminded America that blacks were the "central thread of American history." Blacks were the authentic Americans who pointed redemptively to the incongruity of slavery and democracy, who toiled without compensation to build an economic empire, who suffered mercilessly under the whip and weapon of white masters but continued to pray and sing and trust in the Christ introduced by that master. On this basis, blacks were entitled to the political goods of citizenship, voting, and office holding and to honor and public recognition. In regard to the needs of the black masses, he urged the government to eliminate legal barriers to the advancement of colored people but did not put great trust in its ability to solve the black community's internal problems. The talented tenth of the race had a duty to help solve the problems of black immorality, ignorance, apathy, self-doubt and self-hatred. Black professionals were the unelected representatives charged with responding directly to the needs of the black community.

In this chapter, too brief to do justice to the mind of Du Bois, I have tried to demonstrate the depth and perspicacity of the Du Boisian diagnosis of the psychosocial dilemma of black Americans seeking to merge two selves into a truer self. His twoness description continues to stand as the classic explication of personal transformation among blacks in the twentieth century. I have tried to show that his image of fulfillment combined two prominent features of traditional African-American life—toil and celebration. This image of the strenuous life was in part a reflection of his own life of "hard work and hard play." Finally, I have suggested that his conception of the just society tries to combine, perhaps in a manner too fragile and optimistic for modern sensibilities, the protections guaranteed by America's democratic republic and the humanitarian economic provisions of the socialist welfare state.

All of his life he sought to liberate oppressed blacks and others by challenging them to take responsibility for creating strenuous selves capable of transforming an unjust social order. In this way, Du Bois, like Washington, worked within the African-American tradition of moral thinking. Whereas Washington encouraged a personal ethic of adaptability and subordination to the needs of the dominant society, Du Bois urged upon his audience an ethic of striving and insubordination in pursuit of unfulfilled American ideals.

When Du Bois died in Accra, Ghana, miles separated him, geographically and ideologically, from his people. He knew their plight and culture and was uncomfortable with some of their misdirected goals. Du Bois was too much the prophet, agitator, and vigorous thinker to settle for easy or gradual solutions to the "Negro question." He broke ranks with the Afro-American masses not so much from arrogance as from a deep love for the larger African people and the hope of uniting them. Still, he left behind seminal analytic and historical accounts of African-American life, his bold and often unpopular social strategies, and his poetic gifts to empower and encourage his people in the quest for fulfillment and justice.

3

Malcolm X
and the Defiant Person

When the comprehensive history of African-American triumphs and woes in the twentieth century is written, surely among the most spellbinding and haunting of chapters will be that devoted to the extraordinary young leader we remember as Malcolm X. Until then, his life and thought and death will remain partially shrouded in mystery, and the quest for the authentic Malcolm X will proceed. Many people wonder, Why can we not easily dismiss one whom America wished to erase from life and memory? On what grounds do we claim that he was an effective leader when his public ministry was so brief? Why has there been such fascination with this relatively obscure figure throughout black America since his murder in 1965? A brief answer to all of these questions can be found in Ossie Davis's eulogy. "Malcolm was our manhood," he said.[1] To put it another way, Malcolm was a potent symbol of African-American possibility, a negation of the nigger-destiny scripted by a racist America. We cannot dismiss Malcolm because, like a pulsating, cultural archetype, he lives in the unconscious of every black American. Our quest for the real Malcolm is bound up with the quest for our own better selves. As Davis said to the grieving Harlem congregation and perhaps to all America, "As we honor Malcolm, we honor the best that is in ourselves."[2] Malcolm X has become an African-American icon.

+ The Defiant Person +

In his autobiography, Malcolm recalled the character of his hustler consciousness.

> Looking back, I think I really was at least slightly out of my mind. I viewed narcotics as most people regard food. I wore my guns as today I wear my neckties. Deep down, I actually believed that *after living as fully as humanly possible, one should then die violently.*[3] (Italics mine.)

In that passage Malcolm expressed the general mood of his public life, which I characterize as the *defiant life*. The phrase "out of my mind" is particularly suggestive. Perhaps unintentionally, again Malcolm performed his service as a spiritual physician to black America when he suggested that the street-toughened identity and life-style of his wild and lawless adolescent years was pathological, indeed, pre-psychotic.

No major leader of the twentieth century was better acquainted with the deprivations, seductive pleasures, and repressed potential of ghetto life. As a consequence of this firsthand knowledge, he had an uncanny ability to diagnose the wounded psyche of the urban African American. Having diagnosed it with wit, guile, charm, and gusto, he aimed the awesome force of his mind and voice toward the urban underclass to mobilize fellow wounded souls to claim their personhood.

Peter Goldman, an interpreter of Malcolm's thought, aptly characterizes his ministry in the following passage:

> For the thirteen impassioned years of his ministry, Malcolm X was a witness for the prosecution against white America—a "field nigger," he called himself giving incendiary voice to the discontents of our urban black underclass. Everything about Malcolm was an accusation, his Muslim faith, his militant politics, his self-made manhood, even the name took in token of his renunciation of white society and his embrace of black Islam.[4]

Revisiting Malcolm's life is particularly important in our time, as the ranks of the black, urban underclass swell with alienated youth who are wounded and angry but without acceptable means of expressing themselves. Malcolm can remind the underclass, as he reminds all of America, that oppressed people are redeemable and that black rage and defiance can be constructively used.

+ Biographical Sketch +

Malcolm Little was born in Omaha, Nebraska, in 1925. He was the fourth of eight children of a fragile West Indian woman and a fiery black preacher who embraced both the Baptist church tradition and the secular teachings of the nationalist Marcus Garvey. White vigilantes harassed the Littles out of Omaha, burned their home in Lansing, Michigan, and finally mobbed Malcolm's father, beating him nearly lifeless and leaving him to die under the wheels of a streetcar. The family disintegrated thereafter, and Malcolm wound up in the foster care of a white couple who made him feel somewhat like a house pet. "My presence in that home was like a cat or a parrot or any type of pet that they had. You know how you'll be around whites and they'll discuss things just like you're not there. I think Ralph Ellison calls it the 'Invisible Man' and James Baldwin calls it 'Nobody Knows My Name.' My presence in that home was not the presence of a human being."[5]

Malcolm, stormy and rebellious during this period, dropped out of school as soon as he completed eighth grade, ran away to Boston and later Harlem, and drifted through a series of menial jobs into the zoot-suited, bop-gaited life of a street hustler. Malcolm Little became Detroit Red, then Big Red, dealing drugs, running numbers slips and bootleg whiskey, steering white customers to black brothels, burglarizing homes, and sticking up stores. This lifestyle landed him in Charlestown and then Concord State Prison in Massachusetts. His rapid redemption began in prison with his exposure through family members to Elijah Muhammad's "streettough" theological and ethical teachings. Malcolm embraced Muhammad's historical and self-help instruction with gusto and also expanded his vocabulary and reading skills by copying longhand the entire dictionary under the inadequate light of his jail cell. This habit earned him the scholar's token of the wire-rimmed reading glasses.

Following Malcolm's release from prison, Muhammad was so impressed by his pupil's sincerity, lively mind, and brilliant oratorical and organizing skills that he elevated the novice to the exalted position of national representative of the Honorable Elijah Muhammad and minister of the prestigious Harlem Temple Number Seven.

Malcolm's defiant style and charisma were finally too successful for his own good. His verbal militance agitated not only the white community but also some of Muhammad's inner circle of advisors. Malcolm was officially silenced after characterizing America's practice of violently overthrowing unfriendly foreign governments, which led to the apparent retaliatory assassination of President John F. Kennedy, as a case of "the chickens coming home to roost." He was to remain "silenced" from November 1963 until February 1964, but during this time he received incontrovertible evidence of earlier rumors concerning Muhammad's practice of siring children with a host of young Muslim women. In deep agony, Malcolm left the Nation of Islam but resolved to continue to preach Muhammad's gospel to black people. This resolution changed as he began tutorials in orthodox Islam and then, in April 1964, made his hajj to Mecca—a transforming exposure to the company of white Muslims. Thereafter, Malcolm X preferred to be known as El Hajj Malik el Shabazz, signifying a new self-understanding. Among the masses, this title and name never supplanted their memory of—and psychic need for—the old brother Malcolm X.

Peter Goldman aptly describes his development thereafter as an

> explosive rush from the certitudes of the Black Muslims through a conventional streetcorner black nationalism to a world view of more subtle weave—a shifting and uncompleted blend of orthodox Islam, African socialism, Third World anticolonialism, and that doctrine of racial solidarity known later as Black Power."[6]

During the rushed course of his brief life, Malcolm married one of the sisters in the Nation of Islam, Betty Shabazz, and became the proud father of four daughters. In February 1965, when Malcolm was assassinated at a rally of his fledgling Organization of Afro-American Unity in uptown Manhattan, Betty and the children were present.

+ Conception of Human Fulfillment +

Tracing the development of Malcolm's thought is intriguing because for several years he was not so much an independent agent as the younger member of a symbiotic relationship with an authoritarian surrogate father and teacher. Consequently, no student of

Malcolm X can purchase insight into his life and thought without giving due attention to Elijah Muhammad. As C. Eric Lincoln reminds us, Malcolm "took the teachings of a cult, with all the mythology of the Black Muslims, and universalized them so that black people everywhere, no matter what their religion, could understand them and could accept them."[7] Therefore, I will elaborate Muhammad's understanding of the moral life and note the rare occasions on which Malcolm publicly differed. As we shall see, during his years of loyalty to Muhammad, he ascribed monumental importance to personal discipline and development (religion, culture, and education reinforcing Afro-American exceptionalism) and to economic goods (separate land), which were to be pursued apart from white society. As time passed, Malcolm came to affirm both the complementary importance of political goods as essential for the defiant life and the liberating power of a non-racially exclusive religious faith. Before moving to the substance of his vision of the moral life, however, I wish to place Muhammad, Earl Little, and Malcolm X in the historical and ideological context of black nationalism.

Traditions of Black Nationalism

Black nationalism refers to a body of social thought, attitudes, and actions ranging from simple expressions of ethnocentrism and racial solidarity to the comprehensive and sophisticated ideologies of Pan-Africanism as espoused by Du Bois.[8] Black nationalism is a complex ideological construct incorporating political, cultural, territorial, economic, and religious factors.

In his comprehensive but sketchy study of black nationalism, *The Roots of Black Nationalism*, Rodney Carlisle maintains that this phenomenon constitutes an integral tradition parallel to nationalism among European groups.[9] Nevertheless, he observes that "black nationalists developed ideas, doctrines, and specific plans which have been unique to black nationalism."[10] As compared with other nationalisms designed to evoke loyalty, pride, and a sense of national identity and to develop a sovereign government of a territory, black nationalism's unique features include a special relationship with black Africa and a leadership frequently drawn from the ranks of the clergy.[11]

Carlisle's claim for the uniqueness of black nationalism finds some validation in the biography of the Rev. Earl Little, who was a Baptist minister and a member of Marcus Garvey's UNIA and who embraced its strategy for economic liberation and voluntary racial segregation. With regard to the special relationship to black Africa, we should note that the black American's sense of kinship and solidarity with an entire continent of remarkably varied cultures, tongues, and territories differs from the nation-state-specific, exclusive loyalty typical of European nationalisms. The unwieldiness of a broader continental loyalty underscores the often ambiguous relationship black Americans have had with the peoples, governments, and boundaries of modern, post-colonial Africa. Consequently, solidarity with South African blacks living under a well-defined and familiar system of apartheid has been easier to evoke as an effective rallying point for American blacks.

In order not to overstate the uniqueness of black nationalism, Carlisle calls attention to ten points of similarity among all expressions of nationalism. Nationalists are generally committed to the following goals: a land or territory, a language and culture, common institutions, sovereign government, a common history, love for fellows, devotion to the nation, common pride, hostility to opponents, and hope for the future.[12]

In some form, the Nation of Islam embraced and mediated each of these features and thereby provided Malcolm with a solid nationalistic foundation on which he would later erect a more secularized, Garvey-like version of Pan-Africanism. Black nationalism in general—and the Nation of Islam in particular—was a defiant expression of mass black discontent with America and an earnest attempt to achieve authentic existence in hostile environments. Malcolm X was the most defiant and public oriented of those discontents.

In *Black Nationalism in America*, John Bracey, Jr., August Meier, and Elliott Rudwick observe that nationalist ideologies have been ascendant only in certain historical periods. During four particular periods,

> nationalist sentiment in various forms has been prominent in Negro thought: (1) the turn of the eighteenth century, roughly from 1790 to 1820; (2) the late 1840s and especially the 1850s; (3) the nearly half-century stretching approximately from the 1880s into the 1920s; and (4) since the middle 1960s.[13]

They maintain that:

> In general, nationalist sentiment, although present throughout the black man's experience in America, tends to be most pronounced

when the Negro's status has declined, or when they have experienced intense disillusionment following a period of heightened
but unfulfilled expectations.[14]

The first period was initiated by the waning of equalitarian
enthusiasm inspired by the Revolutionary War. As blacks realized
that they would not be included in the republic, they founded
numerous separatist churches and organizations including the Free
African Society of 1787, the African Methodist Episcopal and various
black Baptist churches, and the Negro Masons. The second period
began with the failure of the antislavery movement of the 1830s and
1840s to liberate the slaves. Disillusionment was fueled by evidence
of racism among many white abolitionists and the growing help-
lessness of the black economic situation. Together with the Dred
Scott decision, these events encouraged the revival of the National
Convention Movement in 1843. At that meeting the Reverend
Henry Highland Garnet urged slaves to kill any master who refused
to liberate them. Moreover, during this period a large number of
black intellectuals committed themselves to colonization whether in
Africa, Central America, the West Indies, or the western frontier
of the United States. Among this leadership class were Alexander
Crummell, Henry H. Garnet, and Martin R. Delany.

The third period commenced with the collapse of the Reconstruction and the gradual deterioration of the Negro's position up
to the turn of the century. The incidence of race riots multiplied in
the North as did lynching in the South. Booker T. Washington's
nemesis, W. E. B. Du Bois, began to express the idea of Pan-
Africanism and delivered an address at the first Pan-African Conference, which was held in London in 1900. After World War I and
the massive northern migration, blacks became urban dwellers in
search of a mediating philosophy to preserve self-esteem and to
insulate them from the pains of economic and racial exploitation.
During the Harlem Renaissance years, a literature and philosophy
regarding the "New Negro" emerged and spread across urban black
America. The "New Negro" was described as a person with enormous
racial pride who advocated racial self-help and solidarity and displayed militance in claiming a rightful place in American society.[15]

The proliferation of nationalist ideologies, which found its most
promising and tragic purveyor in Marcus Garvey, reached a climax

during the 1920s. Garvey was imprisoned and later deported for mail fraud in 1927. From the thirties until the sixties, leading black organizations and spokespersons stressed interracial cooperation, civil rights, and integration. As many blacks were forced to rely on the New Deal in order to survive the Depression and as trade unionists and communists flooded the black communities preaching racial equality and fraternity, the nationalist movement reached another ebb. This brings us to the fourth period, my principal concern in this chapter.

Despite the dominance of an integrationist ideology, the Civil Rights protest of the 1950s produced a distinct and strong strand of black nationalism, represented most visibly by the Nation of Islam. Most interpreters agree that Malcolm X almost single-handedly transformed the tiny Muslim sect into the respected militant wing of the black struggle. As noted earlier, we can gain access to the thought of Malcolm X only through the Nation of Islam and Elijah Muhammad. An adequate appreciation for that organization can best be achieved by viewing it as an expression in the continuous tradition of black nationalism. Because our goal is to clarify the elements of Malcolm X's moral philosophy and teachings, I shall narrow my discussion of the Nation of Islam to its own moral teachings by which Malcolm was resocialized.

Personal Discipline

Both Muhammad and Malcolm X understood personal discipline to be a prerequisite to authentic freedom. Whereas Muhammad advocated discipline as a mode of conformity (to the sect's hierarchy), Malcolm considered discipline to be a form of confrontation (of all unjust structures) available only to thoughtful moral agents.

C. Eric Lincoln, in his oft-cited *The Black Muslims in America*, has observed,

> In their day-to-day living, the Black Muslims are governed by a stringent code of private and social morality. Since they do not look forward to an afterlife, this morality is not related to any doctrine of salvation. It is, quite simply, the style of living appropriate to a divine Black Man in his capacity as true ruler of the planet Earth.[16]

Here, Lincoln's claim regarding salvation seems to reflect a Christian bias wherein the concept of salvation is inseparably linked to some notion of an afterlife or eschaton. However, if we expand our understanding of salvation to include any vision of ultimate human fulfillment and human possibility that is the consequence of divine agency, then we can grant legitimacy to Muhammad's implicit doctrine of salvation.

In *Message to the Blackman in America*, Muhammad explains,

> the prophecy of Habakkuk is true if understood; wherein he says: "Thou wentest forth for the salvation of thy people" (the so-called Negroes) 3:13.
>
> Never before this time did anyone come for the salvation of the so-called Negroes in America, whose rights have been ignored by their enemies (the white race) for 400 years. Now it is incumbent upon Allah to defend the rights of His lost-found helpless people, called Negroes by their enemies. . . .
>
> *I teach not the coming of God but the presence of God, in person.*[17] (Italics mine.)

For Elijah Muhammad and Malcolm, salvation entailed the full enjoyment of freedom, justice, equality, and peace in a territory governed by blacks under the crescent of Islam. For the Muslims, salvation was tantamount to restoration of the original glories of African-Asian civilization. This ancient glory, they argued, could and must be restored on a personal and social level. Muhammad sought to resocialize blacks like Malcolm who had fallen into the "muck" of American racist culture and had become "satans" like their masters. The technology of resocialization was designed to strengthen impulse control and to inculcate discipline, self-confidence, and self-love. In short, becoming a Muslim was tantamount to a triumph of the stronger, superior African over the shrewd, devilish Caucasian. Each black who responded to Muhammad's self-transforming message had to wage a war in his instinctual and psychological life vaguely parallel to the war being waged between colonial European powers and freedom-seeking Africans of the 1950s and thereafter. Although the odds of a black victory seemed slim, with Allah's help the defiant person could overcome weak human nature and emerge a conquerer, a civilized person, a god. Thus, Malcolm and other Muslims were warriors of a sort, slaying their self-hatred and the white Christ of Anglo-American culture, and, in the end, winning salvation that restored them to their former glory.

According to Lincoln, the Muslim code of private morality is one of "rigid discipline, aimed at controlling the total behavior of the individual."[18] The need for such extraordinary self-transformation derives from the fallen condition of the black person who held claim to a rich African past. As Muhammad put it, "We are the mighty, the wise, the best, but do not know it";[19] "It is the knowledge of self that the so-called Negroes lack which keeps them from enjoying freedom, justice and equality."[20]

Muhammad taught his followers to pray five times a day facing east toward the holy city of Mecca and thereby aligned his Lost-Found Nation of Islam with the personal piety of orthodox Muslims. Muslims were forbidden to eat pork and corn bread. These foods not only represented the state of black life in America (poor, unclean, etc.) but also were objectifications of evil; that is, according to the mythology, "hogs possessed all of the characteristics of a white man."[21] By refusing to ingest the flesh of such an undisciplined beast, the black person remained pure in body and spirit at an early stage in his or her development toward divinity. Separation from unclean foods represented a broader commitment to separation from white definitions of the good life.

Muhammad also taught restraint in consumption of permitted meats (lamb, chicken, fish, and beef). He urged his followers to consume one meal per day, as such restraint eliminated physical and mental sluggishness and left more time for industry.

Lincoln observes that "sexual morality is defined in ultrapuritanical terms which are strictly enforced."[22] Divorce is frowned upon but allowed. Women are assigned a somewhat exalted stature in the organization and are not to be regarded as sex objects. The rank and file Muslim "is expected to evince general character traits that can only benefit the society as a whole. Men are expected to live soberly and with dignity, to work hard, to devote themselves to their families' welfare and to deal honestly with all men."[23] Above all, "self-reliance and a sense of mutual responsibility are the hallmarks of Muslim morality."[24]

In one of his strongest proclamations on Muslim morality, Muhammad said,

> The duty of the civilized man is to teach civilization to the uncivilized—the arts and sciences of civilized people and countries of advanced civilization.

> A well-educated, cultured and courteous people make a beau-
> tiful society when it is spiritual. Good manners come from the
> civilized man who does not fail to perform his duty.[25]

Muhammad envisioned an organization and a society inhabited
by refined ladies and gentlemen. In my judgment, this genteel image
of the moral person was too domesticated to suit the tastes of young
minister Malcolm X. Muhammad's methodology for achieving authentic personal and communal life had as its fundamental model
the experience of white Americans, from which he combined the
Puritan ethic, petit bourgeois capitalist programs of economic advance, a success-oriented dress code, and similar concepts. This
paradigm ultimately proved itself insufficient and inappropriate for
the developing social consciousness of Malcolm X.

Malcolm began explicitly to differentiate his image of fulfillment
and his methodology for achieving it after his formal break with
Muhammad in March 1964. Some evidence suggests that he was
skeptical of the methods, if not the goals, of the Nation of Islam
during his tenure as Muhammad's "roving bishop." Journalist and
social critic Louis E. Lomax provided a more informal report on
Elijah Muhammad and Malcolm X in *When the Word Is Given*.
After befriending Malcolm, he enjoyed numerous private conversations, one of which is of extraordinary significance in light of Malcolm's prominent position in the Nation of Islam at the time. Lomax
reports,

> "I'll be honest with you," Malcolm X said to me. "Everybody is
> talking about differences between the Messenger and me. It is
> absolutely impossible for us to differ. What he says is law; that is
> what is done. But I'll tell you this," he added, "Mr. Muhammad
> was with Allah, and he has been granted divine patience; he is
> willing to wait on God to deal with the devil. Well, the rest of us
> have not seen Allah, we don't have this divine patience, and we
> are not so willing to wait on God. The younger Black Muslims
> want to see some action!"[26]

Lomax continues, "For the first, and to my knowledge, only
time Malcolm deviated from the Messenger's position when he said
that."[27] Clearly, Malcolm identified with the impatience and youthful
restlessness of the rank and file and sought to involve them in defiant
public action. Muhammad's perspective was similar to that of a father
who adopted a long-range view and measured his words and deeds

in order to minimize confrontation with the enemy. Indeed, Muhammad acknowledged that whites could teach modern economic practices to blacks and thereby increase the probability of establishing a separate black nation. Malcolm was less sanguine and gracious. His perspective resembled that of an older brother among siblings who feared and loved their father, but waited for the elder brother to provide a safe and appropriate model of relating to him. Malcolm looked at the immediate, short-range context of the civil rights movement as a proving ground for the Nation of Islam. Malcolm felt that the Nation was beginning to lose contact with its mass base and could easily forfeit its status as the militant side of the civil rights movement.[28]

Malcolm found Muhammad's image of the genteel nationalist attractive but situationally irrational and naively conservative. Malcolm was less interested in impressing the white community with a self-reliant black community than in vigorously confronting the white conscience and intellect with the case for justice or violence, liberty or death, "the ballot or the bullet." In order to initiate this confrontational mode of interaction, Malcolm recognized the need for a bolder, more resistant Muslim, one tacitly available for revolutionary violence and self-sacrifice if necessary. During the early years of his ministry, Malcolm accepted Muhammad's insistence on personal discipline and submission in the service of creating group power and public respect. As he matured, however, Malcolm became an advocate of personal discipline and morality as an expression of personal defiance and power, an unshakable ability to resist the crippling forces of injustice and racism.

Having indicated a principal difference in the ideological and strategic perspectives of Muhammad and Malcolm, I now turn to consider other elements of the defiant life. Those elements included economic self-interest, black political power, and a liberating religious faith capable of facilitating the recovery of African cultural wholeness.

Community Economic Self-Determination

During Malcolm's eleven-year tenure as a minister in the Nation of Islam (1952–1963), he was taught to give privileged status to economic goods in the struggle for racial justice and peace. Three points of Muhammad's ten-point "Muslim Program" explicitly articulated claims for economic goods as essential for the fulfillment of the black community and of individuals and for a just resolution of past harms such as slavery and legally sanctioned discrimination. This perspective continued to inform Malcolm's moral and social philosophy during the year of his new direction. By then, however, economic goods had been subsumed under political goods as the proper starting point for advancing public claims for just treatment. Muhammad outlined in his program the following economic goods.

#4 We want our people in America whose parents or grandparents were descendants from slaves, to be allowed to establish a separate state or territory of their own—either on this continent or elsewhere. We believe that our former slave masters are obligated to provide such land and that the area must be fertile and minerally rich.

#7 As long as we are not allowed to establish a state or territory of our own, we demand not only equal justice under the laws of the United States, but equal employment opportunities NOW!

#8 We want the government of the United States to exempt our people from ALL taxation as long as we are deprived of equal justice under the laws of the land.[29]

These provisions (land, jobs, and tax exemption) were sandwiched between demands for freedom, justice, equality, freedom from federal prisons for all "believers of Islam," an end to police brutality, and the prohibition of interracial marriage and integrated schooling. For years, Malcolm proclaimed this agenda as "God's plan," "God's solution," and "justice and compensation for our three hundred ten years of slave labor."[30]

Among the many economic goods they sought, the Muslims earnestly desired land. A racially separate territory was conceived to be an ultimate goal capable of enabling blacks to acquire other nonmoral goods. Segregated voluntarily from whites, blacks could develop culturally distinctive forms of self-government, economic self-reliance and cooperation, and common institutions that affirmed race pride and love for fellow community members.

In the platform of aims and objectives for his fledgling Organization of Afro-American Unity (June 1964), Malcolm noted:

Economic exploitation in the Afro-American community is the most vicious form practiced on any people in America: twice as much for rent for rat-infested, roach-crawling, rotting tenements; the Afro-American pays more-for foods, clothing, insurance rates and so forth. The Organization of Afro-American Unity will wage an unrelenting struggle against these evils in our community. There will be organizers to work with the people to solve these problems, and start a housing self-improvement program. We propose to support rent strikes and other activities designed to better the community.[31]

Following his hajj, other world travel, and the growth of his political sophistication, Malcolm discarded hopes of colonizing America's black population. He realized that there was no place for blacks to go and that the masses were neither interested nor prepared to leave the United States. Malcolm's determination to use conventional civil rights strategies for achieving societal change (boycotts, rent strikes) aligned him with King and other former foes in the movement.

This shift in his thought from romantic notions of possessing a separate territory to sharing limited urban living space reflects not only his maturing pragmatic judgment wedded to a secular understanding of community but also substantiates his repudiation of the more bourgeois economic vision of the Nation of Islam. Interpreter and historian John Henrik Clarke suggests that Malcolm "completely repudiated" the Muslim's "acquisitive thirst for money and property and machine idolatry."[32] "He felt that they were merely imitating the racist enemy. He still believed in separation from his racist enemy, but his was an ideological separation."[33]

On 8 April 1964, during a question-and-answer period at the Militant Labor Forum, Malcolm remarked, "I don't know too much about Karl Marx."[34] He then commenced a quasi-Marxist analysis of America's international economic decline resulting from lost markets and Japanese and European manufacturing superiority. Although he was not a registered Socialist, he shared Marx's contempt for bourgeois consumerism. He even criticized Muhammad for wearing two-hundred-dollar suits while his followers struggled to make ends meet. I concur with Clarke's estimation that Malcolm repudiated the black man's attempt to emulate and surpass the white man in economic rationality. Malcolm was impressed with the apparent happiness and spiritual contentment of poorer, often socialist-governed countries, and he adjusted his view of economic goods in

order to emphasize such modest virtues as simplicity and contentment.

As we observed earlier, Malcolm was socialized by Elijah Muhammad to ascribe priority to economic goods. However, Malcolm's
experience in the arenas of civil rights and international affairs
evinced new emphases in his social and moral thought. To be sure,
economic goods were essential for the fulfillment of blacks and others, but he began to emphasize political goods as the proper starting
point.

Black Political Power

In 1963, during his last year as a member of the Nation, Malcolm
indicated his awareness of potential black political power. In response to a question about birth control (which he understood to
be another white conspiracy to limit the black population), Malcolm
noted, "Already the Negro is the balance of power in any political
election."[35] In his famous speech "The Ballot or the Bullet," delivered
on 3 April 1964, he stated clearly, "the ballot is more important than
the dollar."[36] Two months later, he articulated a more sophisticated
understanding of the relationship between politics and economics,
an understanding that resembles Du Bois's presocialist position.

> Basically there are two kinds of power that count in America:
> economic and political, with social power deriving from the two
> . . . The Organization of Afro-American Unity will organize the
> Afro-American community block by block to make the community
> aware of its power and potential; we will start immediately a voter-
> registration drive to make every unregistered voter in the Afro-
> American community an Independent Voter; we propose to sup-
> port and/or organize political clubs, to run independent candidates
> for office, and to support any Afro-American already in office who
> answers to and is responsible to the Afro-American community.[37]

Malcolm recognized the massive potential of a politically organized and active black community. By urging blacks to register
and vote, he was embracing another conventional civil rights strategy
for change. This posture was a far cry from the condemning prophet
of Temple Number Seven in Harlem who, years earlier, had urged
blacks to withdraw from participating in the white man's government.
Malcolm went on to argue,

> The Negro in this country, before he can win with the ballot, has
> to be made more *politically mature.*

Now many Negroes don't like to be criticized—they don't like for it to be said that we're not ready. . . . We have assets— we have liabilities as well as assets. And until our people are able to go in a closet, put you whites out, and analyze ourselves and discover our own liabilities as well as our assets, we never will be able to win any struggle that we become involved in. As long as the black community and the leaders of the community are afraid of criticism, collective criticism, as a stereotype, no one will be able to pull our coat.

Those whose philosophy is black nationalism are involved right now, and will become involved with any group—green, blue, yellow, pink—that is set up with an organizational apparatus designed to get more of our people involved as registered voters. . . .

Any Negro who registers as a Democrat or a Republican is a traitor to his own people—Registering is all right. That only means "load your gun." Just because you load it doesn't mean you have to shoot it.

Our people need to get registered, need to pile up political power, but they need to hold it in abeyance and throw it when they know that throwing it is going to get results. Don't just throw it because you've got it.[38]

As one would expect, Malcolm's instruction is narrowly conceived in order to mobilize mass political action. If we look carefully, however, Malcolm appears to identify at least four conditions of responsible political action.

First, he affirmed the importance of self-criticism and openness to criticism from people outside of the black community. Second, he advised blacks to develop restraint and political judgment. They could effectively use the ballot as a weapon if they carefully weighed the consequences of voting for particular candidates and refused to vote in an obedient, uncritical manner. Third, he identified a mode of social action that was new even for himself, namely, interracial political coalition building. Finally, he introduced the notion of Pan-African communal loyalty into the voting considerations and behavior of the black community.

In his theoretical discussion of political goods, William Galston observes that "to have a valid claim on citizenship in a community is to meet all the necessary conditions for citizenship."[39] Those conditions include: the ability to act independently and to assume responsibility for one's acts; the ability to articulate one's own interests and to recognize the claims of others; the ability to understand the language, beliefs, history, and institutions of one's community; and finally, a citizen must be loyal to the community.[40] Galston's criteria would seem to reinforce the political judgment and wisdom of Malcolm X in several respects. Both recognize citizenship to be a demanding intellectual and moral obligation. In order to appreciate the degree of courage required for Malcolm to articulate the obligations of citizenship, we must remember that members of the Nation of Islam did not consider themselves to be citizens of the United States. Blacks were victims of America's distorted version of democracy and should in no way consider this country their home. Although Malcolm could not recommend loyalty to an overtly racist and unjust political order, his sharp protests were couched within the context of a profound admiration and faith in democratic, constitutional ideals. And so with pathos he said, "America [today] is the only country in history in a position to bring about a revolution without violence and bloodshed. But America is not morally equipped to do so."[41] He went on to explain that if blacks were

> given what the Constitution says they are supposed to have, the added power of the Negro in this country would sweep all of the racists and the segregationists out of office. It would change the entire political structure of the country.[42]

At that point in his life, Malcolm saw most clearly the radical political potential of a coalition of independent black voters, progressive whites, and other liberal forces in the society. Therefore, the defiant person could participate in the restructuring of American society through informed, cooperative, peaceful action.

Liberating Faith

> The religion that the Honorable Elijah Muhammad is teaching us here in America, today, is designed to undo in our minds what the white man has done to us. It's designed to undo the type of brain-washing that we have had to undergo for four hundred years.[43]

Both during and after his years in the Nation of Islam, Malcolm believed profoundly that Islam was the only religious system capable of providing firm, practical rules for moral living and high self-esteem for struggling blacks. He believed that Islam was able to generate

the "moral reformation necessary to up the level of the so-called
Negro community by eliminating the vices and the other evils that
destroy the moral fiber of the community."[44] Often the purist, Malcolm considered personal moral integrity (purity and honesty) to be
a prerequisite for leadership and participation in civilized society.
Like Du Bois, he charged that Christianity had failed to instill in
blacks a pride in their culture, history, and identity. It had instead
taught blacks to aspire to white American and European values. It
had become an oppressive faith.

For Malcolm and thousands of other young blacks, Elijah Muhammad's version of Islam contained a deconstructive function.
Blacks needed some alternative to the "white American Christianity"
that enslaved them psychologically. Equipped with a liberating faith,
they would be able to love themselves and their fellows and be
empowered to transform an unjust society.

> I feel the responsibility . . . to help you comprehend for the first
> time what this white man's religion that we call Christianity has
> done to us.
>
> I know you didn't expect this. Because almost none of us black
> people have thought that maybe we were making a mistake not
> wondering if there wasn't a special religion somewhere for us—
> a *special religion for the black man.*
>
> Well, there is such a religion. It's called Islam. But I'm going
> to tell you about Islam a little later. First, we need to understand
> some things about this Christianity before we can understand why
> the answer for us is Islam.[45] (Italics mine.)

Malcolm's diagnosis went beyond merely scolding the oppressed
for absorbing the oppressor's religion to confronting them with the
logical question of why they had not considered the existence of a
religion especially suitable for their situation. Blacks were victims
of a propaganda effort to socialize them into becoming innocuous
Christians before they discovered sacred worldviews that allowed,
even encouraged, revolution in the name of God.

Following his hajj to Mecca, Malcolm received his "new insight
into the true religion of Islam."[46] Thereafter, he articulated a more
socially integrative and constructive role for Islam in pluralistic
America. He observed, "America needs to understand Islam, because this is the one religion that erases from its society the race
problem."[47] "True Islam removes racism, because people of all colors

and races who accept its religious principles and bow down to the one God Allah, also automatically accept each other as brothers and sisters, regardless of differences in complexion."[48] The religion of Islam eradicated personal behaviors and attitudes that prevented individual fulfillment and removed the social barriers to multiracial community to make communal fulfillment possible. Whatever other roles religion might serve for humanity, for oppressed people, its primary task entailed the reconstruction of black self-hood, which had been fragmented by the traumas of oppression.

In the first phase of Malcolm's posthustler life, Muhammad's interpretation of Islam helped to liberate Malcolm from vices of the flesh: in his post–Nation of Islam days, orthodox Islam liberated him from vices of the spirit. In the Nation of Islam, blacks were portrayed as the "original race" who created civilization and disseminated knowledge. This suited Malcolm's need for self-esteem for over a decade, but the pilgrimage quickened the pace of his disillusionment with a narrow, sectarian faith. In his brief encounter with orthodox Islam, he discovered the basis for a rational, universal, morally effective liberating faith. Malcolm acknowledged the value of both "moments" of his Islamic faith journey and chose not to disparage Muhammad's ministry among the black underclass. Nevertheless, secretly he knew that this form of faith was only a partial liberation. Ultimately, all blacks should discover their highest identity and loyalties in the universal family of God. He believed orthodox Islam could facilitate this step.

Recovering Africanity

> The social philosophy of Black Nationalism says that we must eliminate the vices and evils that exist in our society, and that *we must stress the cultural roots of our forefathers, that will lend dignity* and make the black man cease to be ashamed of himself. The *restoration of our cultural roots and history will restore dignity* to the black people in this country.[49] (Italics mine.)

Through his speeches and public appearances at cultural arts festivals and the like, Malcolm helped to popularize the efforts of black scholars to valorize the study of African history and culture. Under Muhammad, Malcolm had studied black history vigorously and urged others to appropriate its lessons. As he often said, "History is a people's memory."[50] He believed that blacks would discover the missing and essential component of their self-knowledge by studying African history. He referred to this enterprise as a cultural revolution that would deepen the communal bonds among American blacks while also reinforcing Pan-African sentiments among them. He explained:

> Our cultural revolution must be the means of bringing us closer to our African brothers and sisters. It must begin in the community and be based on community participation. Afro-Americans will be free to create only when they can depend on the Afro-American community for support, and Afro-American artists must realize that they depend on the Afro-American community for inspiration.[51]
>
> A race of people is like an individual man; until it uses its own talent, takes pride in its own history, expresses its own culture, affirms its own self-hood, it can never fulfill itself.[52]

By virtue of his public symbolic role and charisma, Malcolm enjoyed the friendship of movie stars, entertainers, and professional athletes. He was responsible for bringing heavyweight boxing champion Cassius Clay into the the Nation of Islam, where he was reborn as Muhammad Ali. Such proximity to the black glitterati made him sensitive to the plight of black artists who sought to represent the best of black culture. He discovered that these artists were often ignored by the community or compromised by media magnates. Blacks would have to liberate their own artists by supporting their productions. We can infer from his support for independent black artists that Malcolm felt that a fulfilled person would enjoy some active participation in the arts. Indeed, during his hustler days, music, dancing, and using black vernacular English consumed a good deal of his leisure time. However, these "arts" were self-indulging and often socially unredemptive. By contrast, his call for a cultural revolution placed an imperative upon all community members to support noble, high art, a "level" of artistic creativity and excellence that would contribute to the recovery of African modes of perceiving and orienting reality.

Malcolm considered education to be critical for the disciplined, fulfilled life and the recovery of African identity. He was indebted to Elijah Muhammad, who was a strong advocate for education. Item nine of the Muslim program stated:

> We want equal education but separate schools up to 16 for boys and 18 for girls on the condition that the girls be sent to women's

colleges and universities. We want all black children educated, taught and trained by their own teachers. Under such schooling system we believe we will make a better nation of people [*sic.*] The United States government should provide, free, all necessary text books and equipment, schools and college buildings.[53]

Malcolm's profound respect and appreciation for the importance of education derived from his own intellectual awakening in prison. This drama constitutes one of the most fascinating and moving episodes of his autobiography. At the end of the book, he remarked wistfully,

> For the freedom of my 22 million black brothers and sisters here in America, I do believe that I have fought the best that I knew how, and the best that I could, with the shortcomings that I have had. I know that my shortcomings are many.
>
> My greatest lack has been, I believe, that I don't have the kind of academic education I wish I had been able to get—to have been a lawyer, perhaps, I do believe that I might have made a good lawyer. I have always loved verbal battle, and challenge. For instance, I love languages. I wish I were an accomplished linguist. I would just like to study. I mean ranging study, because I love a wide-open mind.[54]

Malcolm became Muhammad's best and most visible specimen of proof that unlettered, poor blacks could overcome their pasts and educate themselves for nation building. If the government could not educate blacks in a manner that cultivated pride and self-respect, then the Muslims would fulfill that public function. The appeal for reparations, then, was to allow the black community to take responsibility for doing what the government was obligated to do but seemed both unwilling and unable to do well. For Muhammad, the historic *Brown v. Board of Education* Supreme Court decision of 1954 was a vacuous symbol that could not provide the kind of educational opportunity blacks needed to become productive citizens.

Emphases in the charter of the Organization of Afro-American Unity were appropriated from Muhammad's educational philosophy.

> Education is an important element in the struggle for human rights. It is the means to help our children and our people rediscover their identity and thereby increase their self-respect. Education is our passport to the future, for tomorrow belongs only to the people who prepare for it today.
>
> Our children are being criminally shortchanged in the public school system of America. . . . The Board of Education of this city

[New York] has said that even with its integration plan there are 10 percent of the schools in Harlem . . . that they cannot improve. A first step in the program to end the existing system of racist education is to demand that the 10 percent of the schools the Board of Education will not include in its plan be turned over to and run by the Afro-American community itself.[55]

Like his teacher, Malcolm advocated community control of education and a nationalist-oriented curriculum specially tailored to the psychological needs of the urban poor. Malcolm dropped Muhammad's conservative insistence on gender separation in the schools. I suspect that he considered this practice to be rather regressive in light of international cultural developments progressing slowly toward sexual equality.

Substantively, Malcolm's vision for education was progressive. He called for schools that would train children to become scientists and mathematicians and for adult education and job retraining programs designed to prepare people for an increasingly automated workplace. Philosophically, he agreed with Du Bois's notion of the special obligations born by fortunate and gifted persons. Malcolm railed against education that instills in black youth merely the worship of diplomas. He argued that "education does not grant special privileges but imposes a duty and an obligation because it is obtained through sacrifice."[56]

Malcolm's vision of the moral life was a patchwork of new and old elements. The foundation of his thought was provided by his own nationalistic father and his surrogate father and teacher. Unremarkable, then, is his affirmation of the importance of personal discipline and integrity, uncompromising commitment to community economic uplift, political empowerment for the underclass, a bold religious alternative to Christianity, and the artistic and intellectual recovery of Africanity. Regrettably, he did not live to add this unusual patchwork to the emerging garment of American life.

+ The Just Society +

Many of Malcolm's reflections on the just society have already been identified in earlier discussions. I summarize them here briefly and move on to his contribution to this conversation. As we shall see, many of his insights follow and reinforce the wisdom and experience of Du Bois.

Over the course of his public ministry, Malcolm's view of the just society shifted away from being racially separatist, parochial, and capitalistic to being universalist, Pan-African, quasi-socialist, and public.

During his years in the NOI, Malcolm embraced Muhammad's utopian vision of a separate black homeland. We should recall from the discussion on Washington's vision of the just society that one of the functions of utopian thought (which Galston elaborates) is to guide concrete political action. Indeed, Washington's insistence upon black voluntary self-segregation and economic self-reliance constitutes a significant and direct ideological link to the visions of Garvey, Muhammad and Malcolm X.[57] The utopian ideal of an African-American zion has been popular in many black nationalist ideologies since the turn of the eighteenth century. It has never been taken seriously by the black majority, who have judged it to be an impractical, risky, and extreme response of desperation to white racism. In light of Marcus Garvey's frustrated effort to colonize large numbers of blacks and Muhammad's apparent personal lack of interest in migrating to Africa or elsewhere, this element of Muslim mythology was doomed to be seen as a hollow wish from the beginning. Subsequent Muslim leaders sought to reinterpret this goal in psychological rather than political terms. Black separation from whites was to be spiritual and cultural, thereby liberating blacks from the historically crippling dependence upon the values and symbols of success in the dominant society. Before Malcolm came to realize this, however, he was captive to a racially exclusive, parochial, and theocratic understanding of the just society.

The African-American Zion was predicated on capitalistic economic practices. Following Muhammad's reasoning, he believed that in the just society blacks should be restored economically to positions of individual wealth enjoyed millennia earlier. Consequently, they espoused notions such as the work ethic, profit motive, competition, private property, incentives, and the free market. Because the principal precondition for a just society was a body of fertile land capable of supporting a thriving population, Muhammad and Malcolm never considered scarcity to be a significant problem. They were certain that the ingenuity of enlightened black farmers and scientists could match any challenge.

With great regret, we must admit that Malcolm did not live long enough to elaborate or give practical shape to his revised vision of the just society. We may infer, however, from statements uttered during that year, some of the primary norms he thought should govern its formation.

Following his travels to Mecca, Africa, and Europe, Malcolm's social perspective began to shift from a separatist to a more inclusive, universalist orientation. He repudiated Muhammad's parochialism, especially his dualistic anthropology, and began to consider all human beings equal before the Creator. A month before his death (January 1965), he espoused the primary norm of equality. In response to the question — "But you no longer believe in a black state?" Malcolm said, "No, I believe in a society in which people can live like human beings on the basis of equality."[58] Clearly, he was firmly committed to the tradition of political democracy and envisioned a society in which blacks and whites could participate in public life together on the basis of mutual respect of citizenship status and political and economic power.

Another significant dimension of his emerging universalist tendencies was the insistence on framing issues of domestic social justice in international rather than national and cultural terms. In 1964 he claimed,

> The entire civil rights struggle needs a new interpretation, a broader interpretation. . . . We need to expand the civil rights struggle to a higher level—to the level of *human rights*. Whenever you are in a civil rights struggle, whether you know it or not, you are confining yourself to the jurisdiction of Uncle Sam. . . . When you expand the civil rights struggle to the level of human rights, you can then take the case of the black man in this country before the nations in the U.N.[59] (Italics mine.)

This ideological shift in thought carried with it tangible tactical benefits. It permitted him, as black America's prosecuting attorney, to bring the black community's case against America before the world court of opinion. The shift represented a more sophisticated comprehension of the nature of global interdependence and justice. Social justice could be defined by norms that transcended national boundaries. Therefore, the just society had to measure up to universal standards of fairness, compassion, and rationality.

Notwithstanding his universalist outlook, Malcolm's social vision maintained a Pan-Africanist agenda and focus. On 11 May 1964, during a visit to Accra, Ghana (Du Bois's final home), he wrote,

> Just as the American Jew is in harmony (politically, economically, and culturally) with world Jewry, it is time for all African-Americans to become an integral part of the world's Pan-Africanists, and even though we might remain in America physically while fighting for the benefits the Constitution guarantees us, *we must "return" philosophically and culturally* and develop a working unity in the framework of Pan-Africanism.[60] (Italics mine.)

The maintenance of a Pan-African bond would be important for blacks as they helped to usher in a just society in America. It would inspire their struggle by linking it to a noble history of African civilization building. Also, it could correct the black community's tendency to misperceive or ignore its own moral significance for other global movements of justice, as well as the tendency to underestimate the number and strength of its global allies. As long as blacks thought of themselves solely as black Americans, they would be doomed to permanent minority status, but, once identified to be exiled Africans in America, they would become part of a global Third World majority.

In addition to the universal equalitarianism and Pan-Africanism of his maturer social vision, Malcolm believed that the just society should distribute its economic resources in a manner that would ultimately eliminate poverty, filth, and hunger. In other words, toward the end of his life, his sympathies for welfare state socialism began to grow. In April 1964, he confessed,

> I don't know too much about Karl Marx, but there was this man who wrote, *The Decline of the West*, Spengler—he had another book that's a little lesser known, called *The Hour of Decision* . . . his thesis is that the initial stages of the world revolution would make people be forced to line up along class lines. But then after a while the class lines would run out and it would be a line up based upon race. Well, I think he wrote this in the early thirties. And it has actually taken place.[61]

One month later, he said:

> They say travel broadens your scope, and recently I've had an opportunity to do a lot of it in the Middle East and Africa. While I was travelling I noticed that most of the countries that have

recently emerged into independence have turned away from the so-called capitalistic system in the direction of socialism. So out of curiosity, I can't resist the temptation to do a little investigating wherever that particular philosophy happens to be in existence.

. . .

The system in this country cannot produce freedom for an Afro-American. It is impossible for this system, this economic system . . . as it now stands, to produce freedom right now for the black man in this country.[62]

Like Islam, socialism seemed to be a system of morality uniquely effective in eradicating the ideology and practice of racism. Although he never approached becoming a doctrinaire Marxist, he was significantly influenced by whites and blacks to view socialism in a calm, rational manner. Malcolm believed that whites who manifested liberal attitudes in race relations were probably influenced by socialism.

In response to the question, "How come neither you nor any of the other leaders ever use the term Socialism as an alternative?" [sic] Malcolm said,

Why speak of it! If you want someone to drink from a bottle, you never put the skull and crossbones on the label, for they won't drink. The same is true here.[63]

This suggests that Malcolm may have been close to advocating socialism to the black community but was hesitant to do so explicitly because of America's paranoia regarding communism and because most blacks were adverse to risking their economic security for an abstract, foreign political perspective. Under the circumstances, Malcolm's cautious, indirect endorsement of the humanistic vision found in some socialist traditions was rational and appropriate.

Malcolm displayed a relentless concern for respecting the human dignity, inherent worth, and potential of the poor. He had risen through the ranks of the ghetto-confined underclass and was living evidence of its untapped intellectual and moral wealth. Wasting such human resources in an economic system designed to reward only the best, brightest, and most selfish persons was a national crime and tragedy. In this respect, both Malcolm and Rawls share the general proposition that society should be so arranged as to reward the effort and excellence of individuals while providing the basic material means for personal development to all persons, whether exceptional in ability or not. I think that Malcolm would find Rawls's difference principle to be a welcome palliative to the harsh and impersonal operations of the market economy. However, Malcolm had clearly lost Muhammad's optimism about capitalism. Peering into a dark future, he sought to envision a socialistic America. At least, he thought, such a nation would provide for its poor and actively seek to eradicate the vestiges of racism.

Malcolm's social analysis gave primacy to race over class as the fundamental reality in world politics and revolution. Racism was not understood to be an independent phenomenon but a function of capitalism. Thus, socialism was conceived to be a nonreligious method for alleviating the "vulturistic" motivations behind racism. Socialism de-emphasized private property and the rapacious drives associated with it that caused capitalists to disrespect the interests of others.

With regard to the manner in which he advanced public claims for allocable goods, we should recall that the Muslims believed that blacks continued to suffer from the effects of past racial exploitation. They believed, as Du Bois did, that blacks were responsible for the economic wealth of the industrial world by virtue of hundreds of years of slave labor. On these bases alone, Muhammad argued that the government was obligated to redress the wrongs of slavery and to fulfill the broken promises of Reconstruction by providing blacks with land holdings in the South. During his NOI years, Malcolm considered the pursuit of a separate land a noble and psychologically important goal for the defiant person. During his year of independent organizing, however, he retreated from this controversial goal and advanced more limited, practical concerns. As we have seen, he demanded that America be true to the rhetoric of equality and fairness in the Bill of Rights and Declaration of Independence.

Finally, Malcolm's social vision was a public one. He appreciated America's pluralistic potential but was disheartened by its lack of interracial communication and tolerance for difference. His rational response, as interpreter Wolfenstein observed, was to "form himself into a two-way medium for honest communication between black and white."[64] Malcolm was committed to and loved free-spirited debate and the art of lively argument. Toward that end, he began to identify a vanguard of whites and blacks interested in creating a more just society and offered himself to be a bridge for cooperation. In February 1965, he said,

> [It would be difficult to get militant whites and blacks together.] The whites can't come uptown too easily because the people aren't feeling too friendly. The black who goes downtown loses his soul. He's in no position to be a bridge because he has lost contact with Harlem. Our Negro leaders never had contact, so they can't do it.[65]

Moreover, Malcolm was acutely aware of forces at work to frustrate the public's awareness of his transformed identity and vision. After his split with the Muslims, he noted,

> One of the major troubles I was having in building the organization that I wanted—*an all black organization whose ultimate objective was to help create a society in which there could exist honest white-black brotherhood*—was that my earlier public image, my old so-called "Black Muslim" image, kept blocking me. I was trying to gradually reshape that image. I was trying to turn a corner, into a new regard by the public, especially Negroes.[66] (Italics mine.)

At the beginning of his ministerial career, Malcolm's defiance was directed toward the white power structure. By the end of his life, much of that defiance was directed toward whites, blacks, and his former organization, indeed, toward anyone who would not accept his protean growth. Malcolm struggled with a complex assortment of ideas that, regrettably, he never formulated into a coherent system.

Notwithstanding his brief period of redirected thinking, he left a legacy maintaining that authentic liberation could not be achieved by focusing exclusively upon the personal transformation of blacks, as did Muhammad. Malcolm argued that white people must change, along with the entire social order. In this important respect, he embodied the best of the African-American moral tradition.

4

Martin Luther King, Jr., and the Integrative Person

Although he died at the promising age of thirty-nine, today he is the best-known African-American in the nation's history. The decades of the fifties and sixties were often chaotic and frenzied, but the movement he led is regarded by many people as the most significant and redemptive moral revolution of the twentieth century. Many powerful individuals in the government viewed him suspiciously and harassed him viciously, but he has become a symbol of virtuous citizenship by which the public behavior of U.S. officials and citizens is now measured and judged.

According to common definitions of saints and heroes, he was neither. In most respects, King was an ordinary person who was gradually transformed by his faith in God and the spirit of his revolutionary times. Therein lies his importance for all of us. His civic and moral achievements and virtues were and are within the reach of ordinary rational people. Personally, he embodied the virtues of liberal Christianity, black folk culture, and the American political tradition of human rights and pragmatism. Symbolically, he was a man for all seasons and people, who managed to combine his African-American cultural and political agenda with his quest for an inclusive, universal human identity. This religious quest for a transcultural community uniquely equipped him to answer the major question implied in his public ministry, "How might blacks discover, in the process of achieving equal justice, their ultimate identities as members of an interconnected, global human family?"

+ The Integrative Person +

In the summer of 1958, King was invited to deliver two devotional addresses at the first National Conference on Christian Education of the United Church of Christ, held at Purdue University. In one of his meditations there, "The Dimensions of a Complete Life," he explicated his vision of fulfillment by using geometry as an organizing paradigm.[1] In this sermon we encounter the skeletal framework of his broad reflections on the moral life. Moreover, this was his favorite sermon, the one he preached as a candidate for the pastorate of Dexter Avenue Baptist Church in Montgomery, Alabama, in 1954, and the one he preached in Westminster Abbey, London, during a visit on his way to Sweden to collect his Nobel Peace Prize in 1964.

Inspired by the geometric perfection of the new city of God described in the Book of Revelation (chapter 21), he suggested that the complete life was analogous to a cube. Each of its three dimensions represents a significant individual commitment. The length of life corresponds to a person's inner concern for his or her own welfare and development, breadth corresponds to concern for the welfare of others, and height refers to concern for reconciliation and communion with God.

In order to demonstrate that King functioned as a pastoral theologian for a broad public and that his vision of human fulfillment was thoroughly public, throughout this chapter I refer to an often overlooked segment of his thought, his "Advice for Living" column published in *Ebony* magazine from August 1957 until December 1958.[2] In those columns, he responded to readers' questions regarding personal and public concerns. They are important because in them we discover a consummate pastoral theologian seeking to respond theologically to a diverse audience in public terms capable of bearing rational, non-Christian scrutiny.

Having surveyed King's published and unpublished writings and speeches, I believe that the metaphor of the *integrative life* adequately captures the underlying vision and mood of the moral life in his thought. I suggest the term *integrative* rather than *integrated* in light of two tendencies in his thought. He conceived the complete life to be a process, a quest rather than an achievement. King was drawn to the German philosopher Georg Wilhelm Friedrich Hegel's notion of dialectical idealism and to wholistic modes of perceiving and orienting reality popular in Eastern religious and philosophical thought. Consequently, he viewed human history as a process of gradual, linear progress resulting from the conflictual interaction of opposing ideas or social practices (thesis, antithesis, and synthesis). Also, he believed that every component of life and reality was inextricably interconnected and interwoven with all other life expressions and forms. Therefore, he viewed the moral life to be an ongoing process in which a person diligently pursues personal balance, harmonic proportion, and moderation among the varied elements of life. The imbalanced life is a frustrated life lived far below its noble and divinely ordained potential for order, beauty, goodness, and purpose.

Some interpreters have assumed that King's graduate school studies in the philosophy of Personalism at Crozer Theological Seminary and Boston University initiated his interest in the person as a crucial element in philosophical and theological reflection. Along with James Cone and others, I maintain that King's early childhood experience of racism predisposed him to study and address the psychological and social effects of oppression on human development. Black church culture has been consistent in its effort to support healthy personal development in a psychologically and physically hostile environment. Because King's fundamental character was shaped and nurtured within the valuing context of the southern, black Baptist church and a stable, black middle-class family, his choice to focus on the personhood of God and humanity in his academic pursuits is unremarkable.

+ Biographical Sketch +

Martin Luther King, Jr., affectionately known as M. L. by his family, was reared in a middle-class, black Baptist home. His family tree included a long line of Baptist preachers and outspoken advocates for freedom and justice. The Kings and Williamses were prominent leaders in the new South. When he was very young, his parents noticed M. L.'s unusual ability to endure pain. Although in obvious pain during spankings, he refused to cry. However, his defenses were not quite prepared for the injury that white America would soon inflict.

In his biography, *Let the Trumpet Sound*, Stephen B. Oates reports King's preschool years, when his closest playmate was a white boy whose father owned the store across the street from the King home. When the two friends entered school in 1935, they attended separate schools. One day, the parents of his friend announced that M. L. could no longer play with their son. Their explanation was, "Because we are white and you are colored."[3] Later, around the dinner table, his parents responded to his hurt by telling him the story of the black experience in America. Historically, through such conversations as this, black youth have been socialized into the protest tradition of the black community and church.

Martin's mother sought to soothe his wounded ego and to reinforce his self-esteem by telling him, "You must never feel that you are less than anybody else. You must always feel that you are somebody."[4] Nevertheless, the sensitive and confidently smart child found the incident very disturbing. King recounted:

> As my parents discussed some of the tragedies that had resulted from this problem and some of the insults they themselves had confronted on account of it, I was greatly shocked, and from that moment on I was determined to hate every white person.[5]

Such racially motivated growing pains could be assuaged and overcome in the therapeutic milieu of the church. Indeed, in the church blacks have always sought to reconstruct reality religiously. At the age of six, King began to sing hymns at local churches and conventions. This was the beginning of a career behind a microphone and before huge audiences, as he tested and refined his oratorical range. He played the violin at fourteen and seemed to relish the change in his voice as a strong adolescent baritone emerged. King asserted that his "greatest talent, strongest tradition, and most constant interest was the eloquent statement of ideas."[6]

Like most black youth in Atlanta, he attended Booker T. Washington High School, where he was exposed to an impressive array of black teachers and school administrators. Still, his years there are remembered to have been academically unremarkable. He enjoyed the usual extracurricular activities of adolescent boys, especially wrestling, dancing, and flirting with girls. Although most of his elders at the Ebenezer Baptist church and in the community knew before he did which college he would attend and which profession he would enter, he enjoyed a relatively carefree youthful life.

Morehouse College had been a fixture in black America since its founding in 1867. It had developed a widely respected reputation for contributing a disproportionate number of black men to the nation's professional ranks, especially doctors, dentists, lawyers, professors, and scholarly ministers. Both his grandfather and father had attended Atlanta's famous college, and King's enrollment there came as no surprise.

Like Washington High School, Morehouse contained a large cadre of outstanding black educators who were role models for their students. While majoring in sociology, King pursued his studies in English, history, and philosophy with noteworthy gusto. At seventeen, he struggled with his own vocational direction as he vacillated between medicine and law. Observing his father over the years, he was quite unsatisfied with the effusive, emotional nature of ministry. He had dismissed ministry completely as a personal option until he met the president of Morehouse, the Reverend Dr. Benjamin Elijah Mays. Mays was a scholarly minister with a Ph.D. from the University of Chicago and a refined capacity to motivate and inspire. Mays demonstrated that a minister could be a rational, moral agent who was socially involved, widely read, and well-spoken. Needless to say, Daddy King was delighted to hear young M. L. publicly acknowledge his intention to become a Baptist minister.

In the spring of 1948, at the age of nineteen, he graduated with a degree in sociology and entered Crozer Seminary in Chester, Pennsylvania. At Crozer, he continued a search begun at Morehouse for a philosophical method to eliminate social evil. He studied the history of philosophy and the thought of Walter Rauschenbusch. In King's first book, *Stride Toward Freedom*, he acknowledged that Rauschenbusch's *Christianity and the Social Crisis* left "an indelible imprint" on his thinking by providing him with a theological basis for the social concern he had developed as a result of his early experiences.[7] As time passed, King read the great thinkers of the East and West, and began to forge a social and moral philosophy

that combined the wisdom of many traditions, especially the cele-
brative and prophetic religious culture of Afro-Americans, the egalitarian political vision of human rights partially elaborated in the
rhetoric of America's founding fathers, and an understanding of
America as a chosen nation received from the Puritan covenant
tradition. He borrowed liberally from all of these and more in order
to construct a public theology that might address all citizens as
members of a single national community.

Social psychologist Allison Davis has observed,

> knowledge of this society was ground into King by his daily ex-
> periences in Atlanta. But between his nineteenth and twenty-fifth
> birthdays, he was educated in a different climate, in university
> classes on religion and philosophy at Crozer, at Harvard University,
> and at Boston University."[8]

In that "different climate," King discovered and experimented
with sources that expressed in academically respectable terms his
emerging social vision and image of the moral life.

Several excellent studies of King's intellectual formation exist,
so I will not attempt to duplicate their perspectives here.[9] Note,
however, that King's formal learning was predicated upon and guided
by the informal learning and personal experience of his early years
in the nurturing matrix of a close-knit black family, church, and
culture. Here, I merely identify some substantive features of the
inchoate theological system that guided his action.

Although he learned much about the power of self-discipline
and nonviolence from his father and extended family, Mohandas
Gandhi embodied the ideal in a socially transformative manner. He
received early exposure to civil disobedience by observing and hear-
ing about the defiance of black people in the South who refused to
conform to Jim Crow laws. Later, he found in Henry David Thoreau
a model and language to legitimate the practice before the dominant
culture. He possessed firsthand knowledge of the social and political
power of the Christian church and found in Rauschenbusch a fuller
elaboration of the prophetic and redemptive mission of the church.
As a sensitive and observant youth, he had learned that social change
always entails conflict, and in the philosophy of Hegel he discovered
the dialectical analysis of history that reinforced his faith in the
future. Although he had observed examples of social evil all of his

life, he found in Reinhold Niebuhr a biblically informed theological analysis of collective sin and evil. Indeed, this understanding of the logic and rhythm of King's informal and formal learning can be applied to all of the major sources he embraced in shaping his own eclectic moral philosophy.[10]

In her autobiography, *My Life with Martin Luther King, Jr.*, Coretta Scott King explained that King had chosen Boston University because he wanted to study the philosophy of Personalism with L. Harold DeWolf and Edgar S. Brightman.[11] This school of thought provided the broad horizon for King's theological, political, and pastoral wisdom. Personalism is founded on the doctrine of the sanctity and inviolability of the person. According to one of the founders of the school, Ralph Flewelling, in religious terms, personalism is theistic, holding that "the person can reach the highest selfhood, the greater his harmony with the Divine nature."[12] Because it is known as the "philosophy of freedom," from a political perspective it holds that society should be so organized as to "provide the best possible opportunity for the self-development of every human being, the basis of all true democracy."[13] Edgar Brightman defined *Personalism* as a "system of philosophy that regards the universe as an interacting system of persons (or selves)."[14] Everything that exists is either a person or some experience, process, or aspect of a person or persons in relation to each other. All of reality is social or interpersonal. Consequently, "a person is taken to be a complex unity of thought and ideal values."[15] King found in this system of philosophy a compelling way of framing human relations to each other, to the world of nature, and to God.

We now turn to consider King's image of human fulfillment or the integrative life. This discussion is organized under the headings of personal integration, civic idealism, economic reformation, integrative education, and Afro-American prophetic Christianity.

+ Conception of Human Fulfillment +

As I noted earlier, the most elaborate and systematic statement of King's vision of human fulfillment is found in his 1958 address to the United Church of Christ. Here we find a sketch of King's thoughts about the formation of moral character. In the language of academic ethics, the vision is an aretaic ethic, an approach to thinking about the moral life and person that focuses on the specific virtues, habits, intentions, and behaviors that good people ought to manifest. Given the seminal importance of that sermon in King's life and for this study, I quote it at length and then attempt to elaborate his understanding of personal integration.

> There are three dimensions of any complete life . . . length, breadth, and height. The length of life . . . is not its duration or its longevity, but it is the push of a life forward to achieve its personal ends and ambitions. It is the inward concern for one's own welfare.
>   . . . the individual is concerned with developing his inner powers. It is that dimension of life in which the individual pursues personal ends and ambitions.[16]
>   The breadth of life is that dimension of life in which we are concerned about others. An individual has not started living until he can rise above the narrow confines of his individualistic concerns to the broader concerns of all humanity.[17]
>   Finally, there is a third dimension. Some people never get beyond the first two dimensions of life. . . . They develop their inner powers, they love humanity, but they stop right here. . . . If we are to live the complete life we must reach up and discover God.[18]

The integrative person creatively balances personal, social, and ultimate concerns. Such people possess a sense of equanimity and moral authority capable of empowering them to take risks for the good of the wider community. King sought to embody this ideal personally. With respect to the personal dimension, we could speak of his excellence as a preacher and orator. He pursued the terminal degree in his field of study and enjoyed developing himself through reading, travel, and interaction with diverse religious traditions, philosophical ideas, literary classics, and cultures. In the social realm we could identify such virtues as altruism and self-sacrifice. He sought to build bridges of reconciliation between persons and groups who were at odds with one another. Although he had grown up in a middle-class family and could have enjoyed a comfortable life-style as a professor or pastor, he committed his life to serving the poor and oppressed, while seeking to nurture his own family. In the theological realm, we could focus on the theological virtues of faith, hope, and love present in his thought and life. He took seriously the notion of "reaching up to discover God." Not content with merely inheriting his "Daddy's" religion, he reached intellectually beyond it into other great world religious classics and traditions to discover the true height and depth of a universal God.

I am persuaded that the ensemble of virtues present in this sketch was integrated into a more comprehensive one that brought together the strengths of all three dimensions. The single virtue that seems to come closest to summarizing King's vision of the integrative life-style is magnanimity. The integrative person possesses the capacity to bear difficulties with patience, to face unjust treatment with a sense of certitude that injustice cannot reign forever, and to forgive and oppose the oppressor while never dehumanizing him or her. Through this virtue we discover the degree of a person's love for self, neighbors, and God. Deficiencies in either realm make living magnanimously difficult, and they remind the individual of his or her need for personal integration.

Perhaps our most bold and memorable images of the young King are those of a calm, dignified, and peaceful gentleman standing courageously against foes of various sorts from racist sheriffs to ravenous dogs. In response to a question regarding the difficulty and efficacy of nonviolence, in his *Ebony* column he wrote:

> It is very difficult to get over a philosophy of nonviolence to people who have been taught from the cradle that violence must be met with violence. But you must somehow continue to follow this way in word and in deed. You must get over to your comrades that the man who does not hit back is the strong man. To return violence for violence does nothing but intensify the existence of violence and evil in the universe. Someone must have sense enough and morality enough to cut off the chain of violence and hate. It is ultimately the strong man who can do this. He who accepts violence without returning it is much stronger than he who inflicts it.[19]

King's suggestion about the person who restrains retributive impulses in the service of a more peaceful universe was an effort to rehabilitate morally the concept of the "strong man" in the black community. In many urban black communities where discrimination and segregation have denied many men the opportunity to meet the conventional expectations of the male role, certain compensatory roles have evolved. Among the host of such roles was the "revolutionary chauvinist." This male role was popular during the civil rights movement. Young people attached high value and honor to socially defiant, angry, articulate, courageous, macho rhetoric and behavior. The more evident these traits, the more highly esteemed their bearer. This role was exemplified by Malcolm X, Muhammad Ali, H. Rap Brown, Stokely Carmichael, and Black Panther leaders Huey P. Newton, Eldridge Cleaver, and Bobby Seale.

In retrospect, the black community has come to recognize that this role was oppressive and patriarchal. Women were not valued as equal partners in the struggle but considered revolutionary only insofar as they submitted to the claims of their male counterparts. We are indebted to black womanist analyses that indicate the ways in which the black power movement was a movement to empower black men but often had little to say specifically concerning the more complex predicament of poor black women.[20]

While organizing in Chicago and other northern ghettoes, King encountered the tenacity and prevalence of the chauvinist ethos. The secular militance of street gang culture and of the black power camp presented profound challenges to King's southern, Christian moral strategies. For militants, the "strong man" was understood to be a fighter despite the fact that this affirmation directly contradicted traditional moral teachings espoused in most Christian churches. Here, King engaged a sensitive spot in the black male psyche. He invited them to surrender macho behavior and self-understanding for the sake of the larger society and world. King placed the heavy burden of self-sacrificing morality on an already oppressed people and thereby sought to transmute their notions of strength. This effort was courageous and often noble but cost him the loyalty of adolescent males who rejected Christian visions of personal fulfillment precisely because such visions were incongruent with the tough realities of urban street life.

In his life-style, King sought to display the virtue of magnanimity in a manner that helped to validate its legitimacy to the masses. On national television, citizens watched the young minister urge an angry Negro crowd to disperse peacefully after his own house was bombed and his family endangered. This image stood in stark contrast to photographs of Malcolm X, who, standing near a window in his household, grasped a rifle presumably waiting for racist intruders. In contrast to such threatening images, King demonstrated that the magnanimous person was authentically strong, whereas Malcolm X posed with weapons that he never used.

Theologically, King identified with Jesus Christ the Suffering Servant, who in his last moments of oppression looked to God and prayed, "Father forgive them for they know not what they do."[21] This Christian image of magnanimity led him on numerous occasions to observe that unmerited suffering could be redemptive.[22] He sought to demonstrate to his followers and to the observing American public that the trauma of oppression could be overcome in a dignified, graceful manner. King appealed to his followers' sense of magnanimity when he reminded them,

> If you will protest courageously, and yet with dignity and Christian love, when the history books are written in future generations, the historians will have to pause and say, "There lived a great people—a black people—who injected new meaning and dignity into the veins of civilization." This is our challenge and our overwhelming responsibility.[23]

Although King did not elaborate systematically the means by which persons came to be integrated and hence able to act magnanimously, his speeches and actions show he believed that by acting magnanimously persons would come to experience personal integration. King urged students and youth to participate actively in the protest marches so that they would learn those revolutionary virtues capable of liberating them and civilizing the social order.

He also believed that this course of action was possible to those who already possessed some degree of personal security and confidence, altruism and self-sacrifice, and faith in God. He knew that in the crucible of slavery the black community had been forged into a magnanimous people. The virtues of long-suffering, resilience, resistance, and compassion were already present within the moral ethos of black culture. Consequently, when he appealed to images such as the Suffering Servant or the Good Samaritan and urged blacks to have morality and sense enough to end the chain of violence and hate, his listeners knew very well what they were being asked to do. As far as Malcolm X and the younger militants were concerned, King asked for too much. Still, King called blacks and other oppressed people to use the strength (soul force) derived from their unmerited suffering in a grand effort to change American society through nonviolence.

Civic Idealism

King believed that moral persons should be concerned not only with the state of their own bodies and souls but also with the moral hygiene of the society. He appealed to all rational, moral persons to support the civil rights movement both because redressing the injustices inflicted upon black citizens was morally right and because extending the goods of democracy to America's largest minority was prudent. In his book *Why We Can't Wait*, he wrote:

> Because Negroes can quite readily become a compact, conscious and vigorous force in politics, they can *do more than achieve their own racial goals*. American politics needs nothing so much as an injection of the idealism, self-sacrifice and sense of public service which is the hallmark of our movement.
>
> One aspect of the civil rights struggle that receives little attention is the contribution it makes to the whole society. The Negro in winning rights for himself produces substantial benefits for the nation.
>
> . . . The revolution for human rights is opening up unhealthy areas in American life and permitting a new and wholesome healing to take place. Eventually the civil rights movement will have contributed infinitely more to the nation than the eradication of racial injustice. It will have enlarged the concept of brotherhood to a vision of total interrelatedness.[24] (Italics mine.)

As King reflected on his crusade in American history, he insisted that the movement was not designed to empower blacks and place them alongside other ethnic interest groups but to transform America's social structure and thereby make of it a model to the world community. If the movement were conceived to be merely the effort of a marginalized group to press group-specific reparations claims on the federal government, then the boundaries of the transaction could be limited to those two parties. If the movement were conceived to be the effort of one community of American citizens motivated by, and faithful to, American traditions of protest in behalf of freedom, justice, and democracy, seeking to seize the conscience of all Americans and compel them to act fairly and compassionately toward these faithful citizens, however, then the movement would have to be understood fundamentally as a far-reaching, public phenomenon.

King was not content to see blacks strive to move into positions of dominance and privilege previously and jealously held by whites.

Rather, he grew to realize that justice required radical transformations within the dominant social structures and distributive institutions of the society. This ethical goal required changes in the way all Americans perceived civic obligation and the commonwealth. We shall have more to say concerning his social justice agenda later.

King was persuaded that African-American loyalty to civic ideals had been demonstrated in costly ways throughout the nation's past. They had fought valiantly in America's wars, resisted the often vigorous recruiting activities of the Communist party, and given their lives demanding full political rights. Notwithstanding the hostile rejection or callous indifference they encountered from the government and the white majority, blacks continued to embrace hopefully the possibility of a just America. King felt that this idealism made blacks exemplary citizens who had earned the respect of their fellow citizens.

King's convictions concerning the presence of civic spirit among blacks were supported by a method for inculcating this virtue in young people. Perhaps his most succinct statement of this was provided in his "Advice for Living" column. Responding to a comment that deplored parental permissiveness in child rearing, King wrote:

> Somewhere along the way every child must be trained into the obligations of cooperative living. He must be made aware that he is a member of a group and that group life implies duties and restraints. Social life is possible only if there exists a balance between liberty and discipline. The child must realize that there are rules of the game which he did not make and that he cannot break with impunity. In order to get all of these things over to the child is often necessary to subject the child to disciplinary measures.[25]

King believed that the child's early socialization in the family was a first lesson in public living that included learning to share space, identifying with group purposes, learning the rules and norms of the group, developing conflict-resolution skills, discovering the appropriate balance between individual freedom and the common good, and recognizing the penalties of breaching the rules of communal life. In light of King's belief that the civil rights movement would inject public virtues into American life, his desire for school-children to participate actively in the struggle is not surprising. Children would benefit immensely from a firsthand introduction to the nature of individual and mass power in a democracy, and they would thereby become part of a long protest tradition that had roots in the black community. Whereas Malcolm X decried the presence of youth on the racial battlegrounds and considered King's involvement of them cowardly, King admired their willingness and relentless passion to march and jeopardize their safety. The youth loved King and would not have responded well to an order of inactivity, and King adored the youthful marchers, although he knew that many would lose their lives in the struggle. He also knew that most would mature into adults who knew the cost of democracy and were willing to struggle for a just society.

A central feature of the integrative life was a commitment to the civic ideals necessary for elevating American life to match the lofty standards contained in the Constitution, Declaration of Independence, and other founding documents.

Interestingly, of the four public moralists in this book, only Du Bois ever ran for elective office. We are left to speculate on King's political directions had he lived longer. Still, he was passionately committed to the goal of adequate black political representation in all levels of government. He argued that blacks must exercise the full range of political goods, especially running for public office. However, his perspective resembled Du Bois's somewhat elitist conception of appropriate public leadership. He observed,

> Until now, comparatively few major Negro leaders of talent and unimpeachable character have involved themselves actively in partisan politics. Such men as Judge William Hastie, Ralph Bunche, Benjamin Mays, A. Phillip Randolph, to name a few, have remained aloof from the political scene. In the coming period, they and many others must move out into political life as candidates and infuse it with their humanity, their honesty, and their vision.[26]

Although he affirmed the moral and political necessity of increasing the number of black elected officials who were intelligent and public-spirited, he realized that the mere presence of such national symbols of hope would do little to change the abject day-to-day economic conditions in which many blacks were trapped, hence the need for the integrative person to focus specifically on personal and societal economic reformation.

Economic Reformation

Like other modern African-American moralists, King was keenly aware of the interdependence of political and economic goods.

He advocated radical economic reform at a societal level and at the level of individual economic behavior. Later in this chapter we will consider the evolution and radicalization of his economic thinking during the last three years of his life.

With respect to personal reformation, King was a strong advocate of the Protestant work ethic and urged blacks to exercise thrift as they began to earn greater wealth. He believed that people should regard their work as a calling from God and should execute their responsibilities with a sense of sacred responsibility and personal pride. He said,

> If it falls your lot to be a street-sweeper, sweep streets as Raphael painted pictures, sweep streets as Michelangelo carved marble, sweep streets as Shakespeare wrote poetry. Sweep streets so well that all the hosts of heaven and earth will have to pause and say "Here lived a great street-sweeper who swept his job well."[27]

Although on the surface King's rhetoric of vocational conscientiousness resembles that of Washington, his understanding of the purpose and meaning of such prescriptions differs from that of Washington. Washington urged vocational discipline and excellence as a means to the end of convincing whites that blacks were worthy of civic privileges. King, however, urged excellence as a religious response of obedience to God's calling and distribution of gifts to people. Both recognized the critical importance of self-esteem for people having the ability and the opportunity to work. King began to advocate full employment as a policy goal for the federal government and businesses.

Always a practical, pastoral theologian, King believed that basic financial habits such as thrift and saving were conditions for the economic liberation of blacks. In the March 1958 issue of *Ebony*, he responded to a reader's question concerning the Negro's responsibility for his or her own financial plight. King wrote:

> There is a great deal that the Negro can do to lift himself by his own bootstraps. Well has it been said by one that Negroes too often buy what they want and beg for what they need. Negroes must learn to practice systematic saving. They must also pool their economic resources through various cooperative enterprises. Such agencies as credit unions, savings and loan associations, and finance companies are needed in every Negro community. All of these are things that would serve to lift the economic level of the Negro

which would in turn give him greater purchasing power. This increased purchasing power will inevitably make for better housing, better health standards, and for better educational standards.[28]

Relative to the social philosophy of Booker T. Washington and Malcolm X, King's advice regarding the economic security of the black community was less progressive insofar as he did not strongly advocate the need for blacks to develop and gain control of manufacturing and industrial corporations. Washington, Elijah Muhammad, and Malcolm X urged blacks to strive beyond their traditional roles in the national economy as consumers in order to become corporate owners and industrialists. This advice was consistent with their vision of economic black nationalism. King was more concerned with the need for an immediate remedy to the crisis of black unemployment, underemployment, and job discrimination.

Rhetorically, he asked,

> What will it profit [the Negro] to be able to send his children to an integrated school if the family income is insufficient to buy them school clothes? What will he gain by being permitted to move to an integrated neighborhood if he cannot afford to do so because he is unemployed or has a low-paying job with no future?[29]

In order to address the institutional dimension of economic oppression, in 1963 King proposed a "Bill of Rights for the Disadvantaged" in order to urge the society to honor its obligation to provide reparations for aggrieved citizens. This bill would utilize the "full resources of the society" to "attack the tenacious poverty which so paradoxically exists in the midst of plenty."[30] One of the ways society could help to restore the black community economically was to commit itself to full employment, an idea he learned from activist Bayard Rustin.[31] Indeed, this was one of the defining features of a just society. Until this economic reformation occurred in society, however, authentically free individuals were called to exercise discipline in their personal economic lives.

Integrative Education

For King, formal education was a potent instrument by which persons could be liberated to become good citizens. He believed that a proper education in civic living could liberate persons from deeply ingrained prejudices, ignorance, and stereotypes. He was convinced that education could achieve at the internal level (attitudes, ideas, feelings) what legislation could not regulate or require.

> Both approaches [are] necessary. Through education we seek to change attitudes; through legislation and court orders we seek to regulate behavior. Through education, we seek to change internal feelings (prejudice, hate, etc.); through legislation and court orders we seek to control the external effects of those feelings. Through education we seek to break down the spiritual barriers to integration.[32]

Before people could live integrative lives, they needed to experience the dismantling of their "spiritual barriers to integration." Educated people should be open-minded, capable of tolerating nonconformists, and able to appreciate variety and plurality in the culture. Indeed, people needed to be educated to understand that to be American meant belonging to a national community of people that consistently cares for its less fortunate members.

King thought that not only should education civilize people but also it should make them productive. Knowledge should be useful, providing skills necessary for modern living. In *Why We Can't Wait*, he bemoaned the fact that masses of poor people "have never learned basic social skills on a functional level—the skills of reading, writing, arithmetic, of applying for jobs, of exercising the rights of citizenship."[33] This lack of preparation for joining the modern, technological system amounted to a new form of slavery and dependence that would not be limited to blacks. He saw that automation was displacing workers and that without certain skills people could not keep pace with advances in the economy. Once they were forced out of their vocations, they could not realize their full potential because their energies were spent on survival.

King believed that the entire society must be mobilized behind public education in order to rehabilitate it. He argued,

> Schools have to be infused with a mission if they are to be successful. The mission is clear: the rapid improvement of the school performance of Negroes and other poor children. If this does not happen, America will suffer for decades to come. Where a missionary zeal has been demonstrated by school administrators and teachers, and where a desire to involve parents, much has been accomplished. But by and large American educators, despite occasional rhetoric to the contrary, have not dedicated themselves to the rapid improvement of the education of the poor.[34]

Because education has been the historic route of social mobility for the poor, King believed that the society had a moral obligation to spend more money and devote more intellectual energy to improving this avenue for progress. In this respect, government initiative was required in behalf of less fortunate persons in order to create the conditions under which they might experience a full, integrative life.

African-American Prophetic Christianity

King was the beneficiary of a family and a church environment that nurtured a socially active understanding of Christian faith and also of a graduate school education that exposed him to the writings of Social Gospel advocates such as Walter Rauschenbusch.

He insisted that authentic Christianity exhibited inclusive, wholistic qualities, disdaining the tendency of some to separate spiritual and material concerns. In his famous "Letter from Birmingham Jail," he observed that "many churches commit themselves to a completely otherworldly religion which makes a strange, unbiblical distinction between body and soul, between the sacred and the secular."[35] Also, he claimed it to be a "fact" that "the gospel of Jesus Christ deals with the whole man—his body as well as his soul, the earthly as well as the heavenly."[36] We should note that King's proclivity to perceive the sacred and secular to be ineluctably intertwined is a common feature of traditional African religious culture.[37] He was bearing faithful witness both to biblical faith and to the African spiritual tradition of which he was a product.

In his first book he presented a fuller, systematic statement of his convictions concerning a wholistic faith.

> Religion at its best, deals not only with man's preliminary concerns but with his inescapable ultimate concern. When religion overlooks this basic fact it is reduced to a mere ethical system in which eternity is absorbed into time and God is relegated to a sort of meaningless figment of the human imagination.
>
> But a religion true to its nature must also be concerned about man's social conditions. Religion deals with both earth and heaven, both time and eternity. Religion operates not only on the vertical plane but also on the horizontal. It seeks not only to integrate men with God but to integrate men with men and each man with himself. This means, at bottom, that the Christian gospel is a two-way road.[38]

For King, African-American prophetic Christianity was rooted in a biblical faith that affirmed the original goodness and divine sovereignty over creation. In light of human sinfulness, however, religion and ethics bore the ongoing task of seeking to reconcile and restore creation to its intended excellence. By asserting this courageously, King challenged the folk beliefs of many black churches and of much southern Protestantism, which devalued life in this cruel world and preoccupied themselves with the "other world." He insisted that looking away from this world in anxious embrace of the next was not an authentically Christian or biblically defensible option in the face of human suffering. He called them to work faithfully and hopefully in order to change people's souls as well as their environmental conditions so that the new souls might be nurtured by new social structures.

This temporal-eternal tension has been a prevalent dynamic throughout the history of Western Christianity. In his classic treatment of this problem, *Christ and Culture*, H. Richard Niebuhr provides a typology that identifies several major traditions of understanding the appropriate relationship between Christianity and civilization.[39] Niebuhr identifies the following traditions: Christ against culture, Christ above culture, Christ of culture, Christ and culture in paradox, and Christ transforming culture. In my judgment, King's prophetic, radical faith places him in the transforming tradition. According to Niebuhr, in the history of this tradition, most adequately represented by Augustine, Christ "redirects, reinvigorates, and regenerates that life of man, expressed in all human works, which in present actuality is the perverted and corrupted exercise of a fundamentally good nature."[40] This orientation led King to observe that

> any religion that professes to be concerned with the souls of men and is not concerned with the slums that damn them, the economic conditions that strangle them, and the social conditions that cripple them is a dry-as-dust religion. Such a religion is the kind the Marxists like to see—an opiate of the people.[41]

As a consequence of this position, King believed that Christian faith was a source for countercultural moral values. The church, properly understood as the living witness of Jesus Christ in the world, was the conscience of the society. As such, the church was to bear witness to the goodness of God's creation, God's love for humanity, and God's destiny for humankind. It would assume a nonconformist stance in the face of ruling class tendencies to abuse the natural environment, to condone hatred and oppression of less fortunate persons, and to deny any transcendant purposes for human existence. This secularized "faith" established the values of materialism, militarism, rabid individualism, and the lust for power. The church is called to resist these forces and to testify to the power of love, unmerited suffering, and the resurrection of the dead.

In addition to its prophetic, transformative function, Christian faith was conceived to be a force for fostering religious tolerance in a pluralistic society. King believed that the features of human existence that all people share in common are of greater consequence than the unique items that differentiate them. This conviction was made evident in his leadership of the civil rights movement. There he sought to unite people of diverse religious, racial, economic, and cultural backgrounds in pursuit of the lofty ideals contained in America's commonly shared, constitutive documents.

King drew upon this faith that fostered tolerance throughout his ministry as he related to various ideological extremes, from secular black power advocates to conservative, white fundamentalists. However, his sophistication in employing this virtue was often most evident in pastoral situations. For instance, in one of his magazine columns, he responded to the following sensitive problem.

> Q: Please help me and my wife to settle our religious differences. My understanding is that a man and his wife are to be as one in everything. I am a Baptist and she is a Seventh-Day Adventist. She goes to church on Saturday and I go to church on Sunday. I don't think that is being as one and I don't think God is pleased.
>
> A: There can be no gainsaying of the fact that it is always a wonderful thing when husband and wife attend the same church. However, when such an arrangement does not exist, the family need not live in continual disharmony. The problem may be solved by concentrating on the unity of your religious views rather than accentuating your differences. There are certain basic points, such as the God concept, the lordship of Christ and the brotherhood of man that all Christians should be united on. Consequently, there can be unity where there is not uniformity. If you and your wife will concentrate on these points

of unity and seek to minimize the ritualistic and doctrinal differences, you will come to see that you are not as far apart in your religious views as it appears to you on the surface.[42]

Skillfully, King introduced a formula, "unity without uniformity," that affirmed the importance of the family unit and of respecting individual preferences. He urged the husband to discover within Christian faith sufficient tolerance to live with difference and to resist chauvinistic temptations to coerce conformity to his religious preferences.

In this instance, King employed consequentialist modes of moral reasoning by positing that a harmonious, peaceful household was the chief nonmoral good that should guide action. For him, the morally right thing to do in such circumstances was that act that would maximize peace and harmony. His advice in this case also provides a clue to his method for effecting cooperation and reconciliation between different Christian communities and between various monotheistic faith traditions. This method is illustrated in another of his columns.

Q: Is Christianity, as a religion, more valid than the tribal religions practiced at one time by Africans?

A: I believe that God reveals Himself in all religions. Wherever we find truth we find the revelation of God, and there is some element of truth in all religions. This does not mean, however, that God reveals Himself equally in all religions.

Christianity is an expression of the highest revelation of God. It is the synthesis of the best in all religions. In this sense Christianity is more valid than the tribal religions practiced by our African ancestors. This does not mean that these tribal religions are totally devoid of truth. It simply means that Christianity, while flowing through the stream of history, has incorporated the truths of all other religions and brought them together into a meaningful and coherent system. Moreover, at the center of Christianity stands the Christ who is now and ever shall be the highest revelation of God. He, more than any other person who has ever lived in history, reveals the true nature of God. Through His life, death and resurrection the power of eternity broke forth into time.[43]

Sensitive to the divisive power of religion, King was at pains to emphasize the integrative, tolerance-inducing potential of prophetic Christianity. At the same time, he understood Christianity to be a force for transforming and challenging persons and institutions.

+ The Just Society +

In the section below, I elaborate what I understand to be the chief elements of King's mature social thought. During the early years of his public ministry in Montgomery, Alabama, his understanding of society and social change was generally optimistic and naive. By the end of his life, his social vision had become quite radical and remained undauntingly hopeful. Before concluding the chapter, we will examine his insights in relation to selected concepts from the work of John Rawls to indicate what King may contribute to contemporary moral philosophy and social ethics.

> The good and just society is neither the thesis of capitalism nor the antithesis of Communism, but a socially conscious democracy which reconciles the truths of individualism and collectivism.[44]

As this quotation reveals, King's integrative vision of the just society synthesized sociopolitical emphases on the self and the community. Traditionally, modern Western thought has conceptualized them as polar opposites. King's intellect resisted such dichotomies, however, and consistently sought to transcend apparent opposites through the dialectical exercise of synthesis and reconciliation.

For King, both systems were inherently flawed but capable of remediation. Communism failed to appreciate and respect the value of individual expression and liberty. By asserting the absolute priority of collective life over the life of the individual, communism found permissible coercing conformity, stifling individual creativity and productivity, and establishing the state as a restraining force in human affairs. Like other Westerners of the period, King was aware of the horrors and excesses committed by the communist regimes of Joseph Stalin in Russia and Mao Tse-tung in China.

Capitalism failed to realize that the authentically free life is profoundly social. By reifying individual rights over against the common good, and denying the interdependence of human life, capitalism encourages egocentric, acquisitive, competitive behavior that tends to compromise the quality of a shared, public experience and community. Capitalist societies permit extraordinary disparities between the haves and the have-nots. In order to legitimate structural economic injustices, various symbols (Horatio Alger) and myths (Protestant ethic of success) are deployed. Then, the economically disadvantaged are encouraged to preoccupy themselves with heroic personal reforms in pursuit of material success and to blame themselves for their lack of advance.

Given these flaws, King was in search of a political economy founded upon realistic and prudent anthropological and sociological insights. The just society must acknowledge the human need for individual freedom in order to achieve and create. It must also acknowledge human potential for self-destruction and the lusts for power and unrestrained pleasure. However, it must also discover the conditions under which meaningful family, community, and national life flourish. The just society must discern the appropriate role of the state in facilitating fulfillment for all of its citizens.

On 4 December 1964, King traveled with an entourage of twenty-six people to Oslo, Norway, to receive the Nobel Peace Prize. On his way, he stopped in London for three days and preached at St. Paul's Cathedral. Unsurprisingly, his sermon was "The Three Dimensions of a Complete Life." Days later he visited Stockholm for a reception held in honor of all the Nobel Prize winners. The visit to the socialist nation left an indelible imprint. Speaking to the SCLC staff in 1966, he reminisced,

> I am always amazed when I go there [Sweden], they don't have any poverty. No unemployment, nobody needing health services who can't get them. They don't have any slums. The question comes to us, why? . . . something is wrong with capitalism . . . there must be a better distribution of wealth, and maybe America must move toward a Democratic Socialism.[45]

During the last three years of his life, King grappled with the problem of economic inequity in capitalist societies. Sweden's democratic socialism persuaded him that the United States could preserve the best of its own political tradition of respecting individual liberty and divinely bestowed natural rights while buttressing that tradition with a more compassionate, inclusive economic system, indeed, some form of socialism. After the trip to Europe in 1964, King's unpublished speeches, more than his well-known writings (portions of which were written by advisors), reveal one central theme—the need to restructure America's political economy in order to achieve a fairer distribution of goods. During this period his analysis of America's crisis shifted from a monocausal focus on race to include class as a decisive variable.

In his last book, *Where Do We Go from Here: Chaos or Community?* he set forth his rationale for restructuring society.

> It is a sad fact that because of comfort, complacency, a morbid fear of Communism and our proneness to adjust to injustice, the Western nations that initiated so much of the revolutionary spirit of the modern world have now become the arch antirevolutionaries. This has driven many to feel that only Marxism has the revolutionary spirit. Communism is a judgment on our failure to make democracy real and to follow through on the revolutions that we initiated. Our only hope today lies in our ability to recapture the revolutionary spirit and go out into a sometimes hostile world declaring eternal opposition to poverty, racism and militarism.[46]

King urged American capitalists to accept the critique represented by communism and to transcend the limitations of both systems by taking up the difficult and delicate challenge of affirming and institutionalizing protection for individual liberty and for the common good. He believed that the United States had abandoned a noble element of its political heritage, yet, given appropriate, courageous leadership, the nation could be led to "recapture the revolutionary spirit" of the founding fathers in an effort to demonstrate America's solidarity with people struggling for freedom in the Third World.

In November 1966, King delivered the Gandhi Memorial Lecture at Howard University. There in the nation's capital, to an audience of elite blacks and whites, he elaborated his focus on class oppression.

> Public accommodations did not cost the nation anything; the right to vote did not cost the nation anything. Now we are grappling with basic class issues between the privileged and underprivileged. In order to solve this problem, not only will it mean the restructuring of American society but it will cost the nation something. . . .[47]

King knew that the government, especially the recalcitrant Congress and President Johnson, would never voluntarily spend the large sums of money necessary for redressing the conditions of the black and white poor. Only massive, dramatic public pressure in an election year would be effective in calling attention to the brewing crisis. April of 1968 was to be the showdown as King led thousands of poor people to Washington, D.C., for an extended campaign of civil disobedience (Poor Peoples Campaign), but as we know, he did not live to return to Washington.

In a keynote address to the National Conference for a New Politics in Chicago on 31 August 1967, he advanced his analysis of the relationship between racism and economics.

> We have deluded ourselves into believing the myth that capitalism grew and prospered out of the Protestant ethic of hard work and sacrifices. The fact is that capitalism was built on the exploitation and suffering of black slaves and continues to thrive on the exploitation of the poor, both black and white, both here and abroad. . . . The way to end poverty is to end the exploitation of the poor. Insure them a fair share of the government's services and the nation's resources. We must recognize that the problems of neither racial nor economic justice can be solved without a radical redistribution of political and economic power.[48]

King recognized that the problem of poverty was complex and could not be blamed solely on the behavior or "culture of the poor" nor on government policies. Both must be transformed for economic justice to become a reality. Consequently, while he preached individual liberty, thrift, and hard work to poor people in order to make them viable actors in the economy, he demanded justice and compassion from political and corporate elites and was prepared to risk his life seeking to effect radical change.

King needed significant courage to debunk popular myths of American innocence and goodness and remind the nation that its wealth rested upon the bones of exploited slaves. Also, he offered a bold example of personal risk taking for the common good by invoking socialist ideals and models of compassionate government following the national hysteria stirred by Senator McCarthy's hatred for communists. Both his historical and political arguments were employed to urge Americans to be true to the noble ideals of the Constitution and Declaration of Independence. If America would not respond to such moral suasion and conscience massaging, however, then the nation would have to prepare to deal with angry, morally serious citizens who would sacrifice their lives in the cause of realizing justice. His rhetoric concerning a radical redistribution

of political and economic power and of restructuring society took
concrete shape in his "Bill of Rights for the Disadvantaged" and in
the "Freedom Budget for All Americans."

The "Bill of Rights for the Disadvantaged" was elaborated in
Why We Can't Wait. King introduced this proposal by arguing that
justice required America to plan "some compensatory consideration
for the handicaps" that blacks had "inherited from the past."[49] He
advanced claims of need and desert or reparations by noting that
response to such claims of distributive justice was inherent to America's political traditions.

> Special measures for the deprived have always been accepted in
> principle by the United States. . . . Throughout history we have
> adhered to this principle. It was the principle behind land grants
> to farmers who fought in the Revolutionary Army. It was inherent
> in the establishment of child labor laws, social security, unem-
> ployment compensation, manpower retraining programs and
> countless other measures that the nation accepted as logical and
> moral.
>
> During World War II, our fighting men were deprived of
> certain advantages and opportunities. To make up for this, they
> were given a package of veterans rights, significantly called a "Bill
> of Rights" . . . In this way, the nation was compensating the veteran
> for his time lost, in school or in his career or in business. Such
> compensatory treatment was approved by the majority of Amer-
> icans. Certainly the Negro has been deprived. . . . This [law]
> should be made to apply for American Negroes. The payment
> should be in the form of a massive program by the government
> of special, compensatory measures which could be regarded as a
> settlement in accordance with the accepted practice of common
> law.[50]

The other concrete plan for achieving economic justice came
in the form of the "Freedom Budget for All Americans." This was
a proposal sponsored by the A. Philip Randolph Institute in January
1967, when Randolph was president of the institute and Bayard
Rustin its executive director. Although King was not the author of
the document, he did write a one-page foreword for the pamphlet
version, which summarizes the full eighty-page text. King wrote,
"The Southern Christian Leadership Conference fully endorses the
Freedom Budget and plans to expend great energy and time in
working for its implementation."[51] The budget was presented as a

practical plan for eradicating poverty within a decade. It identifies seven basic objectives:

1. To provide *full employment* for all who are willing and able to work, including those who need education or training to make them willing and able.
2. To assure *decent and adequate wages* to all who work.
3. To assure a *decent living standard* to those who cannot or should not work.
4. To *wipe out slum ghettos* and provide decent homes for all Americans.
5. To provide *decent medical care and adequate educational opportunities* to all Americans, at a cost they can afford.
6. To *purify our air and water* and develop our transportation and natural resources on a scale suitable to our growing needs.
7. To unite sustained full employment with sustained *full production and high economic growth.*[52]

Galston's distinction between need and desert claims may be invoked usefully here. He observes that "need expresses what we have in common with others, while 'desert' gives weight to what distinguishes us from others."[53] Also, Galston suggests that the "interplay of these two kinds of claims permits us to synthesize the competing experiences of human similarity and difference."[54] This analytic insight helps to illumine the varieties of argument present in King's public discourse.

King's position on allocating goods to deprived black and white citizens reflects a significant and, given a pluralistic society, prudent sense of sensitivity to human similarity and difference. Citing the example of national compensation for military service, King noted that slavery also imposed massive, long-term burdens on black laborers. Unlike military conscription, however, the practice of slavery systematically sought to dehumanize Africans, branded them as genetically subhuman and inferior, and denied them citizenship in a nation they built, all without providing material compensation for their contributions. On the basis of this unique historical experience, he pressed claims of desert that intensified obvious need-based claims. He said, "the moral justification for special measures for Negroes is rooted in the robberies inherent in the institution of slavery."[55] He noted, however, manifesting his inclusive, public habits, that "many poor whites . . . were the derivative victims of slavery," that "to this day the white poor also suffer deprivation and the humiliation of poverty if not of color," and that "while Negroes form the vast majority of America's disadvantaged, there are millions of white poor who would also benefit from such a bill."[56]

The "Bill of Rights for the Disadvantaged" authorized the federal government to mobilize the entire society to attack poverty. He hoped that this might be achieved in large measure through full employment, private-sector initiatives subsidized by the government (especially retention of workers in labor-intensive industries), and a "social work apparatus" designed to inculcate an ethos of independence, work, and self-esteem among the poor. Another interpreter of King's thought, John Ansbro, has suggested that in King's vision of the just society

> industries would be more concerned with persons than with profits, would respect the rights of consumers, and would so improve job opportunities, working conditions, human relations, and the sharing of profits that all workers would be free of a destructive feeling of alienation from their work, their coworkers and themselves. Their governments would concentrate on developing moral power and would arrange to share political power with their citizens.[57]

Interestingly, King was persuaded that the bill and the national climate of compassion that it might induce would "immediately transform the conditions of Negro life." He argued that "the most profound alteration would not reside so much in the specific grants as in the basic psychological and motivational transformation of the Negro."[58] If the United States were to test this claim for one decade, he said, "I contend that the decline in school dropouts, family breakups, crime rates, illegitimacy, swollen relief rolls and other social evils would stagger the imagination."[59]

Clearly, King's faith in federal action and the probability of dramatic positive results were somewhat inflated. Events in the global economy that he foresaw and feared have since come to pass. Tens of thousands of low-skill, high-paying jobs formerly available to black and other heads of household disappeared due to economic decline and relocation to nations with abundant supplies of cheap labor.[60] Congressional and executive initiatives, the Great Society, and the War on Poverty empowered upwardly mobile blacks and women but failed to undermine the behaviors and values that permanently disable most inner city poor people.

If King were present today, he might argue that the nation never took the problem seriously enough to attack it in a sustained, aggressive, and creative manner. Indeed, as many have observed, the war in Vietnam drained energy and resources from the war on poverty. For this reason, I am persuaded that government and citizens are morally obligated to attempt new forms of public and private-sector action to eradicate poverty. Not only is acting now to arrest the expansion of the underclass wise, but also it is politically prudent.

Because King was attentive to ideal visions of society as well as to practical public policy considerations, his thought must be considered in relation to other moral philosophers of American public life. I shall compare and contrast elements in the work of King and John Rawls in an effort to identify features of a more adequate theory of social justice. Specifically, I will focus on two elements of Rawls's theory: the philosophical construct known as the "original position" and the lexical ordering of his two principles of justice.

The enterprise of developing a comprehensive theory of justice for a pluralistic society presents innumerable problems. One of the most basic challenges is to identify principles and practices that do not automatically benefit the interests of certain classes, especially at the expense of other persons. In an effort to manage this problem, Rawls offers a creative interpretation and re-presentation of a familiar concept in modern political philosophy, the state of nature. Searching for the principles of governance that rational persons would select in order to organize a just society, Rawls elaborates a hypothetical situation known as the "original position."[61]

In this situation, individuals are removed from society and faced with choosing principles for ordering a just soceity without knowledge of their own place in that society. Under such circumstances, rational persons would examine the life prospects of every conceivable social position and role to ensure that each represents a humane option. Because no one knows in advance his or her class, race, status, educational level, or natural assets, presumably he or she would select principles of justice that could enjoy wide, if not unanimous, consensus among rational persons.

I am persuaded King would affirm cautiously at least two prominent features of this model: its anthropological correctness and its civilizing capacity. First, one of the significant functions of the "veil of ignorance" is to control for tendencies in human nature that compromise the achievement of a just community. It prevents the institutionalizing of self- and group-aggrandizement at the expense of the society. King's eclectic Protestant understanding of human sinfulness and possibility guided his skepticism regarding overly optimistic proposals for social reform. Based on his personal experience and nurture in a black family and church, his encounters with racism and his formal education as a young adult, especially his reading of Augustine, Paul Tillich, and Reinhold Niebuhr, he was convinced that people were created in God's image but that that image was now distorted due to sin. Sinfulness as an inherent quality of human nature manifests itself in estrangement from God, other persons, and oneself. Consequently, humans long for love, acceptance, and relationship, and they possess reason as a faculty for acquiring them. When this striving assumes a distorted form, selfishness, materialism, and aggressivness are the results.

Although King might view Rawls's general understanding of the force of reason in human nature as too sanguine, he would affirm the intent to which reason is harnessed in the original position. Insofar as Rawls attempts to neutralize greed, rabid individualism, and group-based chauvinism by appealing to the individual's rational self-interest, he operates from a view of human nature and possibility that represents the secular form of a theological anthropology that King held. Rawls's anthropology is accurate in its estimation of both how reason is shackled by self-interest and, notwithstanding, how it may be put to noble ends. In other words, Rawls's interpretation of human existence is fine as far as it goes, but ultimately it is inadequate for helping us to understand both rationality and nonrational dimensions of human experience within nonelite cultures. In order to understand and communicate with such cultures, accounting for the centrality of family bonds, communal values, and religious faith is necessary. Rawls is weak here: King is an authority.

As for the second feature of the construct, King would affirm Rawls's effort to foster the capacity for empathy. As those behind the veil consider the obstacles and opportunities for personal development available in the many available social positions, they are encouraged to develop understanding and compassion for their fellow citizens, an achievement that might not occur in the absence of some creative, role-playing experience. For instance, King would probably approve of adapting this abstract, philosophical exercise into a socially therapeutic form of civic education. As such he might attempt to educate avowed racists (or at least their children) to enter voluntarily the original position wherein they would face the possibility of returning to society as members of a minority group. Presumably, the pupils would discover why the just society must restrain behavior that disrespects non-conformist persons. This therapeutic would help to purify and support the rule of reason in human behavior.

During his public ministry, King anticipated the ends Rawls sought to achieve by developing the original position construct. He did so by encouraging people to develop *experiential* knowledge of how others live. He urged affluent, white college students to join him in marching against racial and economic oppression in the South. He even urged young, black school children to protest segregated schools and to risk their lives while learning what being self-determining citizens meant. King had apprehended both the theoretical and practical dimensions of an adequate theory of justice for a pluralistic society.

Although King would affirm Rawls's thought in these two respects, Rawls invites at least two critiques as well. In particular, Rawls discusses his concept of "reflective equilibrium."[62] He suggests that the principles of justice chosen in the initial situation should accommodate our firmest convictions about justice derived from actual experience and that our judgments should be adjusted according to the ideal principles. This mutually corrective, dynamic praxis approach to theory construction and action is referred to as *reflective equilibrium*.

King might observe that Rawls's anthropology is too thin and that actual historical persons do not behave in the manner Rawls ascribed to those behind the veil. Although King would agree that people are inescapably inclined to be self-interested and that the creation of the political community is the result of these rational calculations, his view of the self is richer and more adequate. Whereas Rawls postulates rational, detached, autonomous, and fully formed persons behind the veil, King's wisdom concerning the inescapable network of mutuality that characterizes human life rings compellingly true. As William Galston observed, "Our separate existences are linked in important ways prior to our application of reason and will to the construction of a common life."[63]

Similar to Du Bois's concerns about the formation of a strenuous self, King was sensitive to the enormous struggle that many blacks experienced trying to be rational and religious in an irrational, immoral milieu. King might urge Rawls to exhibit greater awareness of the thoroughly social character of identity formation. Also, he would instruct him concerning the tragedies (especially racism) that often compromise the process. If Rawls were to heed these suggestions, he might succeed in rescuing this foundational feature of his system from its excessive elitism. As it now stands, apparently only mature, rational (narrowly defined) agents can participate in choosing the principles of justice.

In addition to a thin anthropology, Rawls's solution to what King would identify to be social and structural sin is not radical enough; that is, given the ravages of racism, classism, sexism, and militarism, the principles of justice selected in the original position offer little hope of significant change. Whereas Rawls identifies his task as pursuing clarity about principles of justice and the conditions under which they are apprehended, King calls all persons to the task of creating a radically new society in which reconciliation, mercy, and love are among the public norms ordering the society. King called for a revolution of values and radical restructuring of social institutions. Rawls would seem to be content with much of the status quo, including radical economic inequities if only the arrangement can be made tolerable for the least advantaged. Rawls's principles of justice would be satisfied if the ruling elite would adopt the role of benevolent neighbor or Good Samaritan. King called persons beyond the minimalist claims of principles of justice. He wrote:

> We are called to play the Good Samaritan on life's roadside . . . one day the whole Jericho road must be transformed so that men and women will not be beaten and robbed as they make their journey through life. True compassion is more than flinging a coin to a beggar; it understands that an edifice which produces beggars needs restructuring.[64]

King believed that the concept of love must be introduced into moral philosophical conversation to answer the radical problem of social evil. In the integrative, magnanimous life, love served as the guiding ideal, source of motivation, and the regulating norm that would compel persons, especially religious persons, to take risky action in behalf of eradicating the causes of injustice and not merely treating symptoms. If King's social vision had been limited to fulfilling the demands of procedural justice, probably he would not have spent his public ministry trying to urge the United States and the international community to redirect their energies and resources away from violence toward creating the beloved community. King saw the limits of focusing exclusively on power or procedural justice as the means to achieving the ideal society. Influenced by Paul Tillich's reflections on the relationship among love, power, and justice, King observed, "Power at its best is love implementing the demands of justice. Justice at its best is love correcting everything that stands against love."[65]

In order to produce *lasting* personal transformation along these lines, King believed that a religious conversion must occur. As for societal transformation, he believed that institutions and nations could embrace love as a principle for guiding and judging moral action. In a secularized society, mention of conversion raises eyebrows. Most moderns have been conditioned to experience anxiety and to view with suspicion any sectarian claims. However, King understood conversion in more universal, inclusive terms than did most sectarian leaders. In his last book, he wrote:

> When I speak of love, I am speaking of that force which all the great religions have seen as the supreme unifying principle of life. Love is the key that unlocks the door which leads to ultimate reality. This Hindu-Moslem-Christian-Jewish-Buddhist belief about ultimate reality is beautifully summed up in the First Epistle of Saint John: "Let us love one another: for love is of God: and everyone that loveth is born of God, and knoweth God. He that loveth not knoweth not God; for God is love. . . . If we love one another, God dwelleth in us, and his love is perfected in us."[66]

As a Christian theologian, King was able to draw upon religious resources to address adequately the problem of personal and social evil. To his credit, he was a public moralist who was willing to introduce into moral discourse the controversial but redemptive concept of love.

Having examined Rawls's model of the original position and speculations regarding King's probable response to it, I will consider

Rawls's discussion of the two principles that would be chosen in the original position. In regard to the first principle, Rawls asserts that "each person is to have an equal right to the most extensive basic liberty compatible with a similar liberty for others."[67] This provision is cast in deontological terms so as to indicate that it is non-negotiable. It is an absolute ban against bargaining with basic liberties. In the original position, rational persons would seek to guarantee political liberties against the intrusion of government or of other citizens seeking to maximize their self-interests. In the United States, the spirit of this principle is embodied in the Bill of Rights, the Constitution, and the Declaration of Independence.

King would support this first principle precisely because it is intended to respect the dignity of all persons and to protect individual liberty and human rights from the whims of the majority population. In light of the nation's legacy of racial oppression, he felt strongly that government should function as an ally to nonconformists and minorities.

In the second principle, Rawls asserts that social and economic inequalities are to be arranged so that they are reasonably expected to be to everyone's advantage and attached to social positions open to all persons. Also, the two principles are lexically arranged so that the second is always subordinate to the first.

Given the inevitable inequalities in the real world, Rawls prescribes a formal method (operable in the original position) by which the interests of economically disadvantaged persons may be served. It is known as the *difference principle*, which requires that persons in the original position assume the social position of the least advantaged members of society when examining the effects of social and economic inequalities. If economic inequalities benefit the least advantaged members of society, then they may be considered fair and tolerable. The difference principle requires that inequalities somehow improve the opportunities for personal development among those least favored with natural assets (talent, intelligence, creativity) and material holdings.

This effort to include within his theory of justice a social welfare safeguard for the poor is on its face benevolent and consonant with values in the Hebrew-Christian traditions. However, I am persuaded that King would have raised at least two major objections to his presentation of the principles of justice.

First, during the last three years of his life, King became more intolerant of—and impatient with—the gross economic inequities permitted under capitalism. Despite the humane features of Rawls's proposal, King would challenge him to reject the legitimacy of the yawning chasm separating the economic haves and have-nots. Although the intent of the difference principle is to link the life prospects of the affluent and the impoverished in a trickle-down fashion, we might ask why such class distinctions should be preserved and protected to begin with. By accepting dramatic inequity as a normal feature of a market economy, Rawls aligns himself with the status quo and compromises the appeal of his position for the oppressed.

In keeping with his concern to see a revolution of values, King advocated a large role for government interaction with and coordination of market forces in order to ensure that economic goods were distributed fairly. As we have seen, the "Bill of Rights for the Disadvantaged" elaborated this position most clearly.

The second objection to the two principles that King might have raised has to do with the absolute serial ordering of the two principles. Rawls prohibits any compromise of liberty for the sake of maximizing the nonmoral good. The serial ordering prevents bargaining between the two principles (e.g., forgoing certain political rights in order to maximize economic returns). In an effort to be faithful to the Christian norm of love, King might reject the serial ordering of the principles in favor of a more flexible system that might permit some tradeoffs between the two principles. If circumstances made it possible to benefit substantially the lives of the poor by limiting the full exercise of certain liberties (e.g., the liberty of a labor-intensive corporation to suddenly close shop and move in search of a cheaper labor supply), then King might argue that liberty must always be held in creative tension with the common good. Hence, the appropriate ordering of the principles should be subsumed under the more authoritative guiding norm of love.

King's social vision was profoundly integrative and relational. His understanding of cultural diversity and religious pluralism in the United States was rooted in a sophisticated theological system and not merely a function of pragmatic strategizing. King proclaimed,

> All life is interrelated. The agony of the poor impoverishes the
> rich; the betterment of the poor enriches the rich. We are inev-
> itably our brother's keeper because we are our brother's brother.
> Whatever affects one directly affects all indirectly.[68]

Throughout his public ministry, his action was consistently guided by this biblical and theological conviction concerning the kinship
of the human family.

Moreover, King's social vision was thoroughly and admirably
public, as well as faithful to America's best political traditions. His
claims were never exclusive and divisively sectarian or racially chauvinistic; always they were available for wide public engagement and
scrutiny. He treated the Constitution and other "sacred" texts of
American political culture with deference and employed them as
sources for his public theology. As we have seen, he adopted the
Bill of Rights as a model for his proposal for helping the disadvantaged. In his Nobel lecture, he explained that the nonviolent dem-
onstrators had taken the nation back to "those great wells of democracy which were dug deep by the founding fathers in the
formulation of the Constitution and the Declaration of Independence."[69]

Although he was deferential toward these texts, like Du Bois,
he was grieved by the contradictions between America's promises
of freedom, equality before the law, and inviolable rights on one
hand and the reality of horrific racial oppression on the other. He
identified himself as a custodian (drum major) of the universal revolutionary spirit that energized Thomas Jefferson, James Madison,
Alexander Hamilton, and other activist philosophers. Regarding his
movement, he claimed,

> We feel that we are the conscience of America—we are its troubled
> soul—we will continue to insist that right be done because both
> God's Will and the heritage of our nation speak through our echoing
> demands.[70]

His mission—and the mission of the ongoing movement—was
to remind America of its destiny to become a multiracial, multicultural community of compassion capable of inspiring its global
neighbors to practice love through justice and power wielding. In
order to do this, it must prove that it is capable of granting the goods
of citizenship to nonwhites.

Finally, King possessed a remarkable capacity to communicate his dream, indeed, the nation's dream and destiny, to all rational people. He was a black preacher who became America's preacher. He worked the resources of his southern black Baptist heritage, especially its song, prayer, homiletic, and theatric traditions, in order to make its particular wisdom available to everyone. He was convinced that the black experience of suffering, coping, and transcending or overcoming the traumas of oppression could serve as a socially therapeutic model for the world's struggling people. In presenting his vision of the complete life and just social order, King poignantly exemplified the distinctive wisdom of the African-American tradition of moral thought.

King was one of those remarkable thinkers who comfortably combined liberal philosophy, theology, biblical evangelical faith, insights from the human sciences, and his own black cultural tradition. His was an intellectual eclecticism with integrity forged through activism. This accounts for King's extraordinary and broad appeal throughout the nation and the world.

America's Public Moralists:
Testing Their Visions

We have come to the end of this investigation in African-American moral thought wherein I have examined four major visions of the authentically free person and related conceptions of the just society. In this concluding section, three tasks remain. First, I assess the utility of the selected moral philosophical framework for this study. Second, I critically assess each of the public moralists' visions while comparing them with each other. Finally, I elaborate my case for the relative adequacy of King's moral vision. This judgment is based on King's fidelity to the symbols of Christian faith (especially as they were interpreted in the Afro-Protestant tradition), the rhymes and rhythms of black folk culture (preaching, humor), and the human rights rhetoric of America's democratic tradition. I intend to show that all four moralists were American public thinkers responding to questions with which every major American public philosopher has had to grapple. Although each offered provocative, meaningful answers to these questions, for me King's responses and his unique vision emerge as more public and potentially meaningful for the future of blacks, America, and the world.

The moral philosophical framework that I selected for this study was composed of elements from the writings of John Rawls and William Galston. Although these philosophers disagree in many respects, each contributed important categories and principles that facilitated the organization of this book. Rawls and Galston were most useful in illustrating the kinds of questions a public ethicist is compelled to answer. Here those questions included what I refer to as fulfillment issues and justice issues.

The fulfillment issues have to do with such questions as What is the nonmoral good? What is morally good? What is worth having, doing, and being? Who is a good person? What are the constituent elements and virtues of an authentically free life? and Which goods are required for a fulfilled, moral life? Although each black moralist possessed a different response to the fulfillment issues, each giving emphasis to a particular set of goods, Galston's presentation of basic categories of allocable goods was quite useful for shaping my discussions of these overlapping but diverse substantive agendas. Because the emphases of the four moralists were different, Galston's categories served to remind us that those emphases were expressions of a larger coherent image of human fulfillment in which other goods were not neglected but rather were considered to be subsidiary to some principal good. Galston's categories enabled me to amplify systematically the various distinguishing emphases in their thought and thereby rendered their visions more coherent and attractive as live options for contemporary reflection.

Related to the fulfillment issues were questions of justice, including, What kind of society best embodies the moral ideals of a people? How is the good to be distributed? and On what grounds can people advance claims for certain goods or certain kinds of distributional arrangements? Rawls's overall framework was especially useful for clarifying the relationship between political goods (liberty) and economic goods (standard of living). Rawls reminds us that public philosophers have to take a position relative to the priority of liberty over welfare. His own conviction regarding the priority of the first principle was a provocative example against which the other visions were analyzed. In addition, by virtue of his intent to preserve certain American conventions such as individual political liberties and a free and open economic system, Rawls illustrates one way of incorporating substantive cultural and historical value commitments into moral philosophical theory.

His conception of the original position has potential for helping to reeducate citizens to the duties of civic life and to the power of rationality in public affairs. If this conception could be reformulated into a civic exercise (such as reciting the Pledge of Allegiance or taking the U.S. Constitution exam), then people who embrace a racist perspective might be transformed over time to realize that such convictions are irrational and harmful.

Rawls and Galston should not be understood as models for the black public moralists. None of the black thinkers aspired to become an academic moral theorist. Rather, the two academic philosophers provide a host of conceptual tools (questions, innovative responses and perspectives) that advance and strengthen the substantive agendas of the black moralists. Contemporary black moral thinkers can take advantage of the wisdom collected in the writings and speeches of the earlier moralists as well as the more systematic features of public moral discourse as illustrated in the Rawls and Galston projects.

Despite the differences of perspective and substance between the academic theorists and the public moralists, all of them constitute evidence of an intriguing feature of American life. Regardless of racial identity, cultural loyalty, socio-economic location, and political affiliation, thoughtful people who are socialized in America's political and moral traditions ask similar questions about the human good and how it is to be distributed fairly. American public thinkers have been and continue to be very concerned about the health of America as a national community. They are sensitive to the degree of congruence between American political rhetoric and America's racial and cultural reality. They understand that America is a pluralistic community and that cross-cultural dialogue is necessary for creating a society in which people are recognized and respected. Consequently, the ability to communicate with people outside one's community of origin is an essential capacity for any citizen, not to mention a public moralist or leader. In his own way, each of the moralists proved to be an extraordinary purveyor of the spoken or written provocative word. Moreover, each served as a bridge between the black community and other communities, institutions, and governments.

In this book we have examined in some detail the specific elements of the moral life as they were elaborated by the public moralists. We have also considered their visions of a more just America. In my judgment, their reflections on these two sets of concerns have broad public appeal and merit the attention of a wider contemporary audience. I hope that putting these moralists into dialogue with important academic theorists has advanced the purposes of both communities of discourse. The theoretical framework has helped to show that the moralists and the academic philosophers are involved in a common enterprise and are participating in the same conversation. Although participating at different levels and in varying ways, all of these American public thinkers have applied their energies to shaping and realizing particular conceptualizations of the good life for individuals and larger human associations.

My critical assessment of the four moral and social visions begins with a restatement regarding the markedly diverse life stories of each author. Despite this diversity, these African-American moral thinkers were preoccupied with similar questions and concerns. Washington was born a slave and spent his entire life in the South. Du Bois was born in New England, educated in the South, moved back and forth a good deal between New York and Atlanta, and spent his last years in Accra, Ghana. Malcolm X was born in Omaha but matured in the concrete confines of urban Detroit, Boston, and New York. Martin Luther King, Jr., was born in the South and, after graduating from Morehouse College, pursued his graduate education in the North and later resettled in the South. The two Southerners, Washington and King, resisted the familiar migratory pattern of opportunity-seeking blacks who fled the South for urban, industrial centers. They believed that the South, more than the North, needed their leadership, was familiar to most blacks, and had reaped the most direct benefits from black labor.

As youths, each man seemed to enjoy a warm, affirming relationship with his mother. Of the four, only King's father was present throughout his life. One might speculate that the absence of an accessible father predisposed Washington, Du Bois and Malcolm to search for surrogates and reasonably maintain that General Armstrong, William James, and Elijah Muhammad, respectively became father surrogates who helped to shape their postadolescent vocational directions. Each of the senior partners of these associations functioned as a parallel vocational model for the younger man: Washington became a college president, Du Bois a renowned scholar and professor, and Malcolm the spiritual leader of a new Muslim sect.

We should also acknowledge the probability that Benjamin Mays assumed an identical role in the life of King, however. King's apparent need for a nonparental mentor cautions against the facile assumption that the absence of a father, ipso facto, initiated in each man a search for a paternal role model. Each leader seems to have needed and found a vocational role model who helped to initiate him into the desired profession with advice and affirmation of various kinds. This interaction need not have included the dynamics of transference relative to the father-son dyad. However, quite possibly such dynamics emerged occasionally and served to deepen the bond between them.

When America entered the twentieth century, Booker T. Washington was the foremost spokesman for the former slaves. As much as he desired to, Washington never spoke for all blacks, especially those who were free before the Civil War and the educated black elite in the North. Insofar as he was perceived by the nation to be the principal voice for African-American concerns, however, all competing black voices were compelled to work within the Washington paradigm or explain why they did not. When Du Bois emerged as an ideological rival, a heated debate on political options was launched at every level of African-American society.

Washington understood himself to be the quintessential adaptive person who labored diligently to make himself desirable as a productive community member to all civilized people. The chief virtue of this image—sensitivity to local custom and racial etiquette—was also its greatest vice because the demands of justice could be readily compromised in the service of competing ends such as peaceful, harmonious race relations. Nevertheless, Washington believed that the ends of his strategy justified its weighty costs: the adaptive person who could demonstrate economic value as a productive laborer or merchant would merit the respect and fair treatment that lay at the heart of more militant demands. This was the indirect pursuit of justice.

Fulfillment was conceived to be a fundamentally economic reality. The authentically free person was a property owner, an entrepreneur, a dignified laborer, and one who experienced fulfillment through vocation. Such a person, equipped with the requisite technological capacities or virtues, was prepared to participate as an independent agent in America's commercial arena.

Washington's vision of the good person seemed to rest on the premise that economic self-determination was more fundamental and critical for the constitution of the self than political behavior. One could live well, he seemed to think, without participating in the government of the land, but one could not live honorably without the basic means of providing sustenance for one's family. Economic self-sufficiency was especially important to blacks, he reasoned, because this capacity, as much as self-government, had been disrupted by slavery. Reconstructing the Negroes' sense of confidence in the area of land ownership, household management, and market sophistication was essential before they could participate responsibly in government. Thus, Washington developed a practical moral education designed to cultivate the hand, head, and heart of the freedman. Liberation was an economic achievement, and Washington employed the discourse of partial inclusion in an effort to calm the anxiety of whites and to urge realistic achievements for blacks.

If we remember to assess Washington in his own historical context, we should acknowledge first that he was a very practical, calculating man who conceived of a situationally rational solution to the predicament of the black masses. He shared, after all, their experience of slavery and freedom, and he knew intimately the mind of the southern white as well as the yearnings of most blacks. Washington articulated a strategy for liberation that the common person could realize and charted a course for the masses that was least likely to threaten the majority population and, indeed, might invite their support. According to optimistic capitalists of that day, as blacks became astute in business and generated new products, sales, income, profit, and savings, all Americans would benefit. Washington was the champion of this myth.

If we acknowledge Washington's vision of the person and his social strategy as situationally rational, we must hasten to observe that it was also very likely psychologically injurious, demoralizing, and politically irrational to his followers. He misread the sense of self-confidence among the freedmen who demonstrated their capacities for participation in republican government during Reconstruction. By urging them to ignore explicit political behavior, he unwittingly became an ally to those who argued that blacks were intellectually unfit for civil government. The self-confidence of many blacks was, no doubt, injured by the spectacle of their best-known and trusted leader encouraging them into economic endeavors as if politics were the privileged jurisdiction of whites. Washington's position was politically irrational because it sought to ignore constitutional provisions, the rhetoric of the Declaration, the Emancipation Proclamation, and other American and biblical texts that affirmed the equality of all humans before God and this government. Washington adopted a curious public passivity with respect to the rights specified in the Thirteenth, Fourteenth, and Fifteenth Amendments. His understanding of southern resistance to federal impositions on local customs made him the preferred black leader among whites but also impugned his honesty, courage, and conviction among blacks who took seriously the Constitution and America's other "sacred" texts.

One of the persons who took seriously the constitutive documents of the republic was W. E. B. Du Bois. Unlike Washington, Du Bois refused to accommodate the attitudes of white southerners. He believed that they, like all Americans, should modify their local customs and attitudes to reflect the ideals of the Constitution. The Constitution was the standard for American political behavior, and the Declaration of Independence espoused the values of the republic. One of its principal values is the conviction that all persons were created by God, endowed with inalienable rights, and compelled to participate in their government.

Du Bois believed that voting and political action were essential for authentic freedom and self-fulfillment. The person was conceived to be a self-determining, political agent. The authentically free person was one who, when faced with negative social forces such as racial discrimination, struggled vigorously for justice while maintaining a commitment to humanity in its civilized form. While in the process of struggling against oppression, the strenuous person might dehumanize oppressors, deny their existence as potential community members, and thereby compromise her or his own dignity and humanity. Du Bois believed that the relaxed, disengaged side of the strenuous life would mitigate hate and humanize the freedom fighter. The freedom fighter must continually affirm his or her relation to nature, beauty, the divine, and all humanity. For Du Bois this was accomplished through the arts, literature, and religious participation.

At the center of his vision of the moral life was the image of a citizen in a New England town meeting. The moral person was conceived to be a debater who sought compelling, rational reasons for the structure and function of human associations. The moral person was also conscious of a responsibility for the longevity of the republic. By virtue of status as a citizen, the moral person carried certain obligations to share in the burdens of collective life. By benefiting from the broader public's cooperation, tolerance of differences, and observance of constitutional restrictions on and provisions for individual liberty, the moral person was obliged to make some personal sacrifices for the sake of the whole community.

As Du Bois read the history of America, blacks had always understood the burdens of democracy, the personal sacrifices, and the costs of achieving a just and free community. Thus, he claimed blacks were uniquely qualified to exercise their status as citizens and thereby to renew America's public life and faith in authentic democracy. Rather than restricting the scope of the Afro-American contribution to America's greatness, Du Bois sought to broaden it at the very foundation. Implied in his claim about blacks as authors of an authentic democratic vision for America was the question, To whom does America belong?

He believed that America belonged to people like blacks who truly apprehended America's potential as an inclusive democracy. In contrast, Washington reckoned that America belonged to whites, especially to the entrepreneurial classes, because they were responsible for transforming the North American wilderness into a vast industrial empire.

Toward the end of his long life, Du Bois's energies for demanding inclusion into America waned, and he focused upon the global realities of African independence, Pan-Africanism, and the spread of socialism. He had struggled too long for justice in America, and he would seek inner fulfillment and make a symbolic gesture of reconciliation by returning to the African continent. He moved to Ghana. With that pilgrimage he illustrated the frustration and despair of being rejected in his birthplace and signaled a new African-American agenda for liberation through alliance with the Third World. This was his final tribute to the black nationalist tradition.

Du Bois passed a baton that no one leader or scholar could carry alone. He inspired an entire generation of black historians and social scientists to put their scholarship to politically transformative purposes and modeled for activists an intellectually competent and experience-based style of nationalistic, socialistic leadership. One of the historically significant persons who emerged to carry on the nationalist message was Malcolm X.

Malcolm's early political orientation, largely defined by the Nation of Islam, was similar to Washington's despair of American electoral politics and his emphasis on land, wealth, and material acquisition. As the defiant Malcolm was educated and discovered the distribution and structure of power in America, his focus shifted to subsume economic goods under the more fundamental political goods. Washington never made such a public shift, although he secretly supported efforts to enfranchise blacks.

Malcolm's vision of the authentically free person was informed by the revolutionary spirit of African freedom fighters and of Thomas Paine and other American patriots. The defiant person was ever poised to resist—violently if necessary—any act that might have the effect of disrespecting one's human rights. Because the person was conceived to be inviolable and sacred, Muslims were obliged to counteract offenses swiftly and harshly.

Although the early Malcolm and Washington agreed on the primacy of economic goods for authentic freedom, Malcolm's broader vision of the moral life was more militant and uncompromising than Washington's. This active, strenuous dimension of his vision situates it much closer to that of Du Bois. Whereras Du Bois managed conceptually to juxtapose the Apollonian and Dionysian forces in the authentic life, however, Malcolm was almost obsessed with rigorous, Spartan discipline. Malcolm's defiant vision seemed to leave little place for play and lighthearted relief.

After his hajj and the launching of his own organization, Malcolm allowed for aesthetic outlets such as plays and concerts. The simplicity and hard, narrow rationality of his earlier Spartan vision was moderated to acknowledge the importance of the arts in African culture and personality.

With respect to the question of the ownership of America, Malcolm would note that the nation rightfully belonged to native Americans who were victimized by European conquests. He also noted that now the nation belonged to the white community, which employed force and deception to possess the land. The young Malcolm was convinced that, under any scenario, America was not the country of or for black people.

Like the mature Du Bois, Malcolm grew to understand the complex, interconnected relationship between politics and economics and sought to keep both arenas in view as he struggled for justice. When he was killed, his unfinished agenda included fostering African and African-American dialogue and exploring socialist economic arrangements in the Third World. However, Malcolm's contribution to black nationalism and to the civil rights movement at this level was not original or far-reaching, as Du Bois had nurtured the Pan-African movement and committed himself to a socialist and communist agenda before Malcolm was born. Malcolm's contribution to both traditions lies in the skill with which he advanced the black nationalist "separation motif" but with an eye toward expanding opportunities for blacks in the mainstream of American society.

Martin Luther King, Jr., in many ways stood tall above his predecessors because he was able to learn from them and, figuratively, to stand on their shoulders and strengths without duplicating their errors. He learned from the excesses and shortcomings of his forerunners, but he also explicitly criticized their visions of authenticity. He was impressed by Washington's sincerity in his belief that the South eventually would respond to the needs of Negroes, especially after Negroes demonstrated their readiness for citizenship rights. However, he contended that Washington's message of passive acceptance of an unjust system was evil because it constituted cooperation with that system. King's inner dialogue with Washington convinced him that bold, noncooperative action must be taken in order to challenge the structures of oppression.

King expressed admiration for the scholastic achievements of Du Bois, especially those represented in the book, *Black Reconstruction in America*.[1] He affirmed Du Bois's mammoth contributions in resurrecting black history and revising American history. He also concurred with Du Bois's emphasis on higher education. However, King expressed dissatisfaction with the class elitism of the early Du Bois who advocated special educational opportunities for the talented tenth. Himself a member of the black leadership aristocracy, King was suspicious of any scheme that might allow the best and brightest to benefit while leaving behind those of modest achievement and ability. King's inner conversation with Du Bois yielded a pride in the African-American contribution to American democracy but also renewed King's Christian commitment to serving the poor and least advantaged population, which included whites as well as blacks.

King praised Elijah Muhammad and Malcolm X for their rehabilitative successes with ex-convicts, dope addicts, and other hopeless, victimized persons. They succeeded where psychologists, sociologists, and penologists had failed. However, King adamantly rejected the Muslims' law of retaliation toward white aggressors. He reaffirmed that Jesus taught the moral superiority of love over self-destructive violence. King's conversation with Malcolm sensitized him to the anger and despair of northern, urban blacks but also deepened his conviction about the necessity of interracial cooperaton in the struggle against racism. Also, Malcolm helped King to see the civil rights movement in its global context, which led both to refer to it as a human rights movement.[2]

King's achievement lies in the comprehensive, pluralistic, public, and Christian character of his moral thought. The symbols, ideas, actions, and discourse he synthesized were distinctly and faithfully American. Consequently, King emerges as the most widely accessible of the African-American thinkers in this book. As a public thinker who can be appropriated by many diverse communities in America, King's personal and social visions of fulfillment and justice have their proper place within a long tradition of American reflections on personal and public morality.

Unlike the visions of the other thinkers, which cohered around discrete sets of goods that could be identified as economic in Washington's case, political in Du Bois's case, and interrelated economic and political goods in Malcolm's case, King conceived of the authentically free life in more comprehensive terms. In his vision of a complete life, political, economic, personal developmental, and recognition goods and virtue had their proper places. Although he advocated a comprehensive, wholistic, and integrated personal vision, his conception was not a static, aesthetic ideal. King's ideal could be achieved only on the run by people who were diligently and actively pursuing excellence and justice.

King's vision reflects elements of the other positions. We can detect in King's praxis Washington's adaptive effort to cooperate with persons of all races, Du Bois's strenuous effort to name the African-American contributions to America's greatness and to struggle against the oppressors without dehumanizing them, and Malcolm's defiant witness in behalf of the downtrodden victims of democracy. Moreover, King self-consciously sought to go beyond them and to be more comprehensive and inclusive in his vision, strategies, and appeal. King's comprehensive, simple, elegant vision of the complete life avoided excessive emphasis on a particular category of goods and claimed a place for all of the goods in an orderly, systematic framework.

King's moral vision possessed a sophistication that emerged from dialogue with rather diverse symbolic resources. Clearly, he took seriously the positions of rival black thinkers, learned from them, and offered to them his honest criticisms. More than the others, however, King investigated and incorporated the wisdom of other religious, philosophical, humanistic, and cultural traditions. His vision of the complete life and just community represented a synthesis of insights from several sources, including the Hebrew prophets, the New Testament, the founding fathers, Kant, Hegel, Marx, Walter Rauschenbusch, Gandhi, Niebuhr, Thurman, and the Personalists.[3]

King's methodological eclecticism was an expression of a deeper theological conviction about the interrelatedness and solidarity of the human family. Because all people were creatures of God, adequate knowledge about God and reality could be acquired best by learning from each culture, and a multiracial, multicultural community was the most appropriate symbolic expression of God's creativity and unity. Although each of the black thinkers resisted provincialism and traveled and read widely, King was more self-conscious about learning from and incorporating diverse traditions, especially Eastern ones.

King's pluralistic perspective enabled him to speak to a broad audience in terms with which many could identify. This was not an opportunistic, token effort to patronize other cultural groups but an honest effort to indicate his respect and tolerance for the multiform manifestations of human wisdom.

Related to the claim that he was a true pluralistic thinker is the contention that King was a public thinker. In his public utterances, whether "Letter from a Birmingham Jail," his famous speeches, or his "Advice for Living" columns, ample evidence supports the judgment that King self-consciously spoke to all rational people, sought to appeal to their consciences, and had a vivid understanding of the character and possibilities of the nation's public life.

Given the nation's racial paranoia at the time, Washington resigned himself to operating as a black voice, although he enjoyed numerous friendships with affluent whites. Consequently, his vision of a democratic America was somewhat truncated and based on a model of white domination and continued black submission. His conception of authentic personal freedom was designed to accommodate the inequities of American public life. He thought blacks would be better to experience fulfillment in one realm of modern life and accept other social limitations than to demand full inclusion but not realize any genuine power or tangible progress. His principal audience was the black community, although most of his brokering put him before respectable white audiences.

The early Du Bois worked diligently to speak to all rational and receptive minds. His unique function was to bear witness to the Enlightenment in the African-American community. However, he understood himself to be a spokesman for the Negro race not by virtue of abundant shared experience as much as by the duty incumbent on the elite of the minority group. His enormous intellectual and communicative prowess, together with his refusal to accommodate injustice, enabled him to build many bridges of racial cooperation, especially during his years as editor for the NAACP. Du Bois was a public thinker who appealed to a wider audience than Washington, in some measure as a function of his broader education and different formative life experiences.

Du Bois's image of the strenuous life, an African-American adaptation of William James's concept, could appeal to nonblacks, although some features of the black experience could not be fully appropriated or emulated by others. At the end of his life, Du Bois lost faith in America's possibilities as an exemplary just society precisely because the nation could not settle the nagging problems of the color line. Also, he perceived that Christianity was uncritically reinforcing white supremacy and class domination. Thus, Du Bois fully committed himself to a socialist, black nationalist, Pan-African

agenda that compromised his public appeal. Even many blacks preferred the earlier Du Bois of the *Crisis* magazine period who agitated
in behalf of a multiracial society. Indeed, he gave up on America
before the black masses were persuaded to follow his direction.

Malcolm X thought of himself as the quintessential voice of the
black masses. He railed against the Washingtonian accommodations
of the established black leadership and, over against them, asserted
his dramatic, messianic, and drastic solution to the American dilemma. Indeed, during the middle and late sixties, separatist and nationalist expressions captured the imaginations of an increasingly
large and diverse black clientele.

For the most part, the early Malcolm did not address the white
community or seek to transform faulty thinking, purge racist attitudes, and evince compassionate behavior toward blacks. According
to Elijah Muhammad's carefully calculated therapeutic strategy, Malcolm presented the moral turpitude of whites with ruthless indig-
nation while simultaneously elevating the self-esteem of blacks.

Malcolm's defiant image of fulfillment was tailored for the black
experience, although he recognized parallels in the experience of
Jews and other European immigrants. Malcolm did not imagine the
possibility of authentic liberation in the United States until the last
months of his life. After the break with Muhammad, and his hajj,
he acknowledged the impracticality of achieving absolute separation
from American values and culture. Even then, Malcolm remained
skeptical about the prospects for blacks assimilating into the nation's
life and urged voluntary self-segregation and local control of community institutions. His vision accommodated the local control of
community institutions. His vision thereby accommodated the realities of race and power in America.

More than his forerunners and colleagues, King was deliberate,
consistent and exemplary in his effort to be a public theologian. He
understood himself to be a product of the black church and the
history of African people in the New World but not as a voice for
blacks alone. His understanding of the transformative life possibilities in the gospel and of the economic nature of oppression led him
to conceive of the human race as his parish. He viewed all social
existence as inseparably intertwined and thus was obliged to minister
to the human spirit wherever he encountered people.

His special genius was an ability to assimilate the core insights and symbols from various traditions and to combine and enliven them within the inherited art form of the black Baptist sermon. The sermon structure was so well-defined that he was obliged to make explicit references to the spiritual heritage of Jewish and Christian traditions, but it was flexible enough to permit him to engage in political and philosophical discourse. Masterfully, King brought them all together, Plato and Augustine, Gandhi and Freud, and bellowed forth profound ideas to common listeners who often did not comprehend the depth of his message. Still, they listened because they loved the preaching and the credible presence of the young preacher.

King employed the sermon form in public space and thereby subtly transformed a pluralistic audience into a momentary congregation that shared basic political and moral values—a civil religion. Seeking to engage people at the intellectual, emotional, and behavioral levels, he appealed to the religious visions and values that gave rise to America. He sought to give a prophetic cast to the nation's civil religion by making racial tolerance a moral obligation. The good citizen was necessarily open-minded and tolerant of nonconformists.

Finally, King was more faithful to the symbols and message of Christian tradition than were the other figures of this book. This adherence was important because the Christian tradition, and specifically the Bible, was the foundational resource for the African-American community in its drive from slavery to freedom. The Bible contained Jewish stories of bondage and liberation that were appropriated and creatively adapted by African slaves. It also contained testimonies of how Jesus cast his lot with the oppressed of society. Black people have always approached this sacred scripture from an appreciative and critical perspective. The black church is one of the rare traditions in the modern world that takes scripture seriously for shaping its view of reality and moral living and neither abandons the authority of the Bible nor drifts into literalistic and combative fundamentalist habits of mind.

In the twentieth century, black leaders who have failed to be appreciative as well as critical in treating the Christian tradition have immediately sacrificed their mass appeal. Washington attacked the churches for their economic naivete but affirmed the virtues of practical, demythologized religion. His stature in the black Christian community was generally high, as evidenced by his frequent presentations at national black church conventions, but somewhat compromised by his obvious lack of enthusiasm for traditional black religion.[4] Du Bois severed his relationship to the black church community early in his career and chose instead to study it and, later, to criticize folk faith along the lines of Washington's admonishments. His commitment to communism further widened the chasm between his vision for liberation and the hearts of the waiting masses. Malcolm's rejection of Christianity, which he characterized as the white man's religion, together with his strident black nationalism, antagonized most black clergy across the nation.[5] Malcolm often displayed a sense of moral and religious superiority vis-à-vis Christians who had failed to speak effectively to the underclass and the prison population.

Washington, Du Bois, and Malcolm X loved black people and worked untiringly for their liberation. However, they all compromised their influence among the majority of blacks because they failed to galvanize grassroots support among the masses who continue to embrace a distinctive version of Christianity as normative for daily living. Although I am compelled to express respect and admiration for the courage they displayed in differentiating themselves from the black Christian tradition, intellectual honesty requires that we make judgments about the effectiveness of their alternative positions. Indeed, these alternatives helped to distance them from the spiritual and metaphorical center of black life.

More than the others, King understood the tenacity and liberating potential of the Christian message for black Americans. He mined the treasures of the Bible, the Constitution, and the Declaration of Independence and aptly applied them to the struggle of the masses. As they listened, they were convinced that the God of ancient Africa and of biblical revelation was present in history and working for their authentic freedom. They were empowered by the knowledge that they were not solely oppressed people but also the people of God. As they were God's people, America was God's experiment. King believed that the soul of America was an unclaimed and contested treasure belonging to those who offered the most noble vision of its moral possibilities. America had the potential to become the first nation to respect and empower poor, common people. As a public prophet, King was determined to remind America of its vocation.

In differing degrees, Washington, Du Bois, Malcolm X, and King embraced and appealed to constitutional values and concepts. As we have seen, however, King espoused those values more consistently, effectively, and persuasively. On the basis of this faithful but critical and corrective embrace of American political ideals and symbols, he stands out as the most significant and useful for our national life.

Returning to the tasks I outlined at the beginning, I would summarize by noting that I have demonstrated that each figure was a serious thinker as well as an effective activist. Each advocated an implicit image of fulfillment around which a host of goods and virtues were organized. I have shown that their reflections on the moral life and social justice are important and cannot be dismissed as trivial or ignored any longer. A reconsideration of their writings can enrich contemporary theological and social scientific investigations into African-American life.

Also, I have indicated the public character of the thought and intentions of the moralists and argued that King emerges as the most compelling and significant public moralist for our time and the foreseeable future. Each of these moralists envisioned a nation in which the rights and dignity of all people would be respected. Their understandings of the just society owed much to American political ideals. They recognized the need for white America to live up to the promises of the Constitution by accepting the full participation of blacks in public life. They also recognized that an oppressed, marginalized people would require a distinctive sort of resocialization into the mainstream of the nation's life. Through the organizations they founded or led, each leader sought to prepare blacks to claim their portion of the nation's goods and in the case of King, to help America radically reorder its priorities. As public thinkers, in differing degrees they sought to teach blacks and whites their mutual obligations as members of a single, diverse society. They wanted American citizens to practice civility.

Finally, we have demonstrated the useful, albeit limited, function of employing categories from contemporary moral philosophy.

William Galston and John Rawls have helped to clarify and illustrate the structure of a public philosophy and thereby facilitated the systematic presentation of African-American moral thought.

This is an exciting period for black theology and political philosophy in North America. The genre has matured beyond mere impassioned reactions to theology written by whites. Today, exciting work is being born of mutual dialogue and criticism among black and Third World theologians, womanists, feminists, Marxists and progressive white theologians. A new course has been charted by leading black thinkers. They recommend revisiting the classics of African-American religion, literature, and popular culture in an effort to discern the theologies, moral and nonmoral values, coping strategies and social criticism inherent in the tradition. This book commends special attention to African-American wisdom about personal fulfillment and social justice. My hope is that the emphasis on societal change typical of early black theology will be balanced now by attention to methodologies of personal transformation. Personal and social change are inseparable components of authentic and lasting liberation.

+ Notes +

Introduction

1. Parker Palmer, *The Company of Strangers: Christians and the Renewal of American Public Life* (New York: Crossroad, 1981), p. 73.

2. None of the recently published comparative studies of these and other black leaders elaborates systematically their reflections on the constitutive elements of the moral life. Rather, each concentrates on the social philosophy, political praxis, and/or theological orientation of one or more of these figures and gives little or no attention to their guiding conceptions of human fulfillment. See Peter Paris, *Black Leaders in Conflict* (New York: Pilgrim Press, 1978); Anne Wortham, *The Other Side of Racism* (Cleveland: Ohio State Press, 1981); John Hope Franklin and August Meier, eds., *Black Leaders of the Twentieth Century* (Urbana: University of Illinois Press, 1982); Allison Davis, *Leadership, Love and Aggression* (New York: Harcourt Brace Jovanovich, 1983).

3. Peter Goldman, "Malcolm X: Witness for the Prosecution," in *Black Leaders of the Twentieth Century*, ed. John Hope Franklin and August Meier (Urbana: University of Illinois Press, 1982), p. 306.

4. William Galston, *Justice and the Human Good* (Chicago: The University of Chicago Press, 1980); John Rawls, *A Theory of Justice* (Cambridge: Harvard University Press, Belknap Press, 1971).

5. Rawls, *Theory of Justice*, p. 92.

1. Booker T. Washington and the Adaptive Person

1. Louis R. Harlan, *Booker T. Washington: The Making of a Black Leader, 1956–1901* (New York and London: Oxford University Press, 1972), p. viii.

2. Booker T. Washington, *Up from Slavery* (Garden City, N.Y.: Doubleday & Company, 1965; reprint, *Three Negro Classics*, with an introduction by John Hope Franklin, New York: Avon, 1965), p. 148.
3. Harlan, *Making*, p. 109.
4. Ibid., p. 3.
5. Ibid.
6. Ibid.
7. Ibid., p. 15.
8. Ibid., p. 29.
9. Ibid., p. 34.
10. Ibid., p. 98.
11. Ibid., p. 103.
12. Ibid., p. 196.
13. Samuel R. Spencer, Jr., *Booker T. Washington and the Negro's Place in American Life* (Boston: Little, Brown & Co., 1955), p. 41.
14. Ibid., p. 33.
15. Harlan, *Making*, p. 52.
16. Spencer, *American Life*, p. 36.
17. Louis R. Harlan, "Booker T. Washington and the Politics of Accommodation," in *Black Leaders of the Twentieth Century*, ed. John Hope Franklin and August Meier (Urbana: University of Illinois Press, 1982), p. 4.
18. Spencer, *American Life*, p. 140.
19. Ibid., p. 183.
20. Ibid.
21. Washington, *Up from Slavery*, p. 147.
22. Harlan, *Making*, p. 5.
23. Booker T. Washington, *Selected Speeches of Booker T. Washington*, E. Davidson Washington, ed. (Garden City, N.Y.: Doubleday, Doran & Co., 1932), p. 11.
24. Ibid., p. 16.
25. Ibid., p. 42.
26. Booker T. Washington, *The Story of My Life and Work*, Louis R. Harlan, ed., The Booker T. Washington Papers, vol. 1 (Urbana: University of Illinois Press, 1972), p. 62.
27. W. E. B. Du Bois and Booker T. Washington, *The Negro in the South* (New York: Citadel Press, 1970), p. 49.
28. Harlan, *Making*, p. 4.
29. Washington, *Selected Speeches*, p. 89.
30. Ibid., p. 90.
31. Booker T. Washington, *The Negro in Business* (Boston: Hertel, Jenkins & Company, 1907).
32. Washington, *Selected Speeches*, p. 19.
33. Booker T. Washington, *The Story of the Negro*, 2 vols. (London: T. Fisher Unwin, 1909), 2:192.

34. Booker T. Washington, quoted in John Hope Franklin, *From Slavery to Freedom*, 3d ed. (New York: Vintage Books, Random House, 1967), p. 392.
35. Franklin, *From Slavery*, p. 393.
36. Ibid, p. 395.
37. Washington, *Up from Slavery*, p. 296.
38. Ibid., p. 322.
39. Franklin, *From Slavery*, p. 396.
40. Ibid.
41. Harlan, "Booker T. Washington," p. 15.
42. Ibid.
43. Franklin, *From Slavery*, p. 396.
44. Washington, *My Life and Work*, p. 113.
45. Washlngton, *Selected Speeches*, p. 44.
46. Washington, *Up from Slavery*, p. 138.
47. For an excellent examination of the formation and nature of slave religion, see Albert Raboteau, *Slave Religion* (New York and Oxford: Oxford University Press, 1978).
48. Sydney E. Ahlstrom, *A Religious History of the American People* (New York: Doubleday, Image Books, 1975), p. 589.
49. Washington, *Story of the Negro*, 2:355.
50. Washington, *Selected Speeches*, p. 150.
51. Spencer, *American Life*, p. 35.
52. Washington, *Up from Slavery*, p. 249.
53. Washington, *Story of the Negro*, 1:13.
54. Ibid., 2:271.
55. Ibid.
56. Harlan, *Making*, p. 194.
57. Ibid.
58. Ibid.
59. Ibid., p. 195.
60. Ibid.
61. Ibid., p. 196.
62. Ibid., p. 197.
63. Ibid.
64. Washington, *Selected Speeches*, p. 19.
65. Louis R. Harlan, *Booker T. Washington: The Wizard of Tuskegee, 1901–1915* (New York and Oxford: Oxford University Press, 1983), p. 174.
66. Ibid., p. 199.
67. Washington, *Selected Speechs*, p. 15.
68. Ibid., p. 48.
69. Ibid., p. 94.
70. Galston, *Justice and Human Good*, p. 14.
71. Ibid., p. 15.
72. Ibid., p. 16.

73. Washington, *Selected Speeches*, p. 115.
74. Ibid., p. 50.
75. Ibid., p. 100.
76. Rawls, *Theory of Justice*, p. 60.
77. Ibid., p. 61.
78. Washington, *Selected Speeches*, p. 52.
79. Ibid.
80. Harlan, "Booker T. Washington," p. 10.
81. Washington, *Selected Speeches*, p. 78.
82. Ibid., p. 80.
83. Ibid., p. 83.
84. Ibid., p. 80.
85. Ibid., p. 84.
86. Galston, *Justice and Human Good*, p. 5.
87. Ibid., p. 197.
88. Ibid., p. 5.

2. W. E. B. Du Bois and the Strenuous Person

1. W. E. B. Du Bois, *Dusk of Dawn*, quoted in Elliott Rudwick, "W. E. B. Du Bois: Protagonist of the Afro-American Protest," in *Black Leaders of the Twentieth Century*, ed. John Hope Franklin and August Meier (Urbana: University of Illinois Press, 1982), p. 63.
2. W. E. B. Du Bois, *The Souls of Black Folk* (New York: Signet Classics, New American Library, 1969), p. 54.
3. W. E. B. Du Bois, *W. E. B. Du Bois Speaks 1890–1919*, 2 vols., Philip Foner, ed. (New York: Pathfinder Press, 1970), 1:79.
4. Du Bois, *Souls*, p. 45.
5. Ibid.
6. W. E. B. Du Bois, *Dusk of Dawn* (New York: Harcourt, Brace & Co., 1940), p. 7.
7. Du Bois, *Souls*, p. 94.
8. W. E. B. Du Bois, *The Gift of Black Folk* (New York: Washington Square Press, 1970), p. 178.
9. Ibid., p. 30.
10. Du Bois, *Du Bois Speaks*, 1:71.
11. Arnold Rampersad, *The Art and Imagination of W. E. B. Du Bois* (Cambridge: Harvard University Press, 1976), p. 170.
12. Ibid., p. 170.
13. Du Bois, *Dusk*, p. 241.
14. Ibid., p. 303.
15. W. E. B. Du Bois, *The Autobiography of W. E. B. Du Bois: A Soliloquy on Viewing My Life from the Last Decade of Its First Century* (New York: International Publishers Co., Inc., 1968), p. 6. Both *Darkwater* and *Dusk of Dawn* were more essays on the concept of race as illumined by his own life than conventional autobiographies. See Herbert

Aptheker's editor's preface in *Autobiography* for Du Bois's attitude toward autobiographies.

16. Ibid., p. 58.
17. Ibid., p. 71.
18. W. E. B. Du Bois, *Darkwater: Voices from Within the Veil* (New York: Schocken Books, 1920), p. 11.
19. Du Bois, *Dusk*, p. 14.
20. Du Bois, *Autobiography*, p. 92.
21. Rampersad, *Art and Imagination*, p. 10.
22. Du Bois, *Autobiography*, p. 89.
23. Rampersad, *Art and Imagination*, p. 5.
24. Ibid., p. 6.
25. Ibid., p. 7.
26. Du Bois, *Autobiography*, p. 114.
27. Ibid., p. 108.
28. Ibid., p. 133.
29. James identified three constituents of the self—the material self, the social self, and the spiritual self. See *The Principles of Psychology*, 2 vols. (Toronto: Henry Holt & Co., 1890; reprint ed., New York: Dover Publications, 1950), pp. 292-315. He explained that "the body is the innermost part of the material self" but also includes our clothing, family, home, and property (p. 292). The social self was conceived to be the recognition one gets from one's friends. James explained that "a man has as many social selves as there are individuals who recognize him and carry an image of him in their mind" (p. 294). The spiritual self was conceived to be one's "inner or subjective being . . . psychic faculties or dispositions . . . [which are] the most enduring and intimate part of the self" (p. 296).

    In a fascinating discussion of the "rivalry and conflict of the different selves" under a subsection by the same title, James called attention to the impossibility of actualizing all of our competing empirical selves. As a solution to this problem, he suggested that "to make any one of them actual, the rest must more or less be suppressed. So the seeker of his *truest*, strongest, deepest self must review the list carefully, and pick out the one on which to stake his salvation" (p. 310). James also suggested a hierarchical arrangement of the different selves, a process that involved a "direct ethical judgment" based on the worth of the various selves and other social considerations (p. 315).
30. William James, *Faith and Morals* (New York: Meridian Printing Company, 1962), p. 211.
31. Don Browning, *Pluralism and Personality* (Lewisburg, Pa: Bucknell University Press, 1980), p. 281ff.
32. Du Bois, *Dusk*, p. 56.
33. W. E. B. Du Bois, *The Philadelphia Negro* (1899, reprint, New York: Schocken Books, 1967).

34. Du Bois, *Dusk,* p. 58.
35. Du Bois, *Autobiography,* p. 256.
36. W. E. B. Du Bois, *Prayers for Dark People,* Herbert Aptheker, ed., (Amherst, Mass.: University of Massachusetts Press, 1980), pp. vii–xi.
37. Ibid., p. viii.
38. Rampersad, *Art and Imagination,* p. 85.
39. Du Bois, *Souls,* pp. 871–91.
40. Ibid., p. 52.
41. Ibid., p. 197.
42. Du Bois, *Du Bois Speaks,* 2:38.
43. Ibid., 2:39.
44. Du Bois, *Gift,* p. 65.
45. Ibid., p. 67.
46. Du Bois, *Dusk,* p. 41.
47. Ibid., p. 47.
48. Du Bois, *Du Bois Speaks,* 2:80.
49. Ibid.
50. Ibid., 2:82.
51. Rampersad, *Art and Imagination,* p. 164.
52. Du Bois, *Du Bois Speaks,* 2:85.
53. Ibid., 2:84.
54. Rampersad, *Art and Imagination,* p. 164.
55. Du Bois, *Dusk,* p. 141.
56. Du Bois, *Du Bois Speaks,* 2:113.
57. Ibid., 2:114.
58. lbld., 2:230.
59. Ibid., 2:87.
60. Ibid., 2:93.
61. Du Bois, *Dusk,* p. 62.
62. Du Bois, *Souls,* p. 211.
63. Ibid., p. 222.
64. Ibid.
65. W. E. B. Du Bois, *The Seventh Son: The Thought and Writings of W. E. B. Du Bois,* Julius Lester, ed. (New York: Random House, 1971), 1:575.
66. Du Bois, *Prayers,* p. 63.
67. Du Bois, *Du Bois Speaks,* 1:98.
68. Ibid.
69. Ibid.
70. Du Bois, *Souls,* p. 213.
71. Ibid., p. 214.
72. Rawls, *Theory of Justice,* p. 60f.
73. Du Bois, *Darkwater,* p. 144.
74. Du Bois, *Du Bois Speaks,* 2:87.
75. Ibid., 2:298.

76. Ibid., 2:310.
77. Ibid., 2:307.
78. Ibid., 2:309.

3. Malcolm X and the Defiant Person

1. Ossie Davis, eulogy delivered at the funeral of Malcolm X, February 1965, Brooklyn, New York.
2. Ibid.
3. Malcolm X, *The Autobiography of Malcolm X*, with the assistance of Alex Haley (New York: Grove Press, 1964), p. 453.
4. Peter Goldman, "Malcolm X: Witness for the Prosecution," in *Black Leaders of the Twentieth Century*, ed. John Hope Franklin and August Meier (Urbana: University of Illinois Press, 1982), p. 305.
5. Ibid., p. 307.
6. Goldman, "Witness for the Prosecution," p. 310.
7. C. Eric Lincoln, *The Black Muslims in America* (Boston: Beacon Press, 1961).
8. John Bracey, Jr., Elliot Rudwick, and August Meier, eds., *Black Nationalism in America* (Indianapolis: Bobbs-Merrill, 1970), p. xxvi.
9. Rodney Carlisle, *The Roots of Black Nationalism* (Port Washington, N.Y.: Kennikat Press, 1975), p. 1.
10. Ibid.
11. Ibid., p. 2.
12. Ibid., p. 4.
13. Bracey et. al., *Black Nationalism*, p. xxv.
14. Ibid.
15. Ibid., p. xiiv.
16. Lincoln, *Black Muslims*, p. 80.
17. Elijah Muhammad, *Message to the Blackman in America* (Chicago: Muhammad's Temple, 1965), p. 5f.
18. Lincoln, *Black Muslims,* p. 161.
19. Muhammad, *Message*, p. 32.
20. Ibid., p. 31.
21. Lincoln, *Black Muslims*, p. 81.
22. Ibid., p. 82f.
23. Ibid., p. 83.
24. Ibid.
25. Muhammad, *Message*, p. 44.
26. Louis E. Lomax, *When the Word Is Given* (Cleveland: World Publishing, 1963), p.105.
27. Ibid., p. 106.
28. Eugene Victor Wolfenstein, *The Victims of Democracy* (Berkeley and Los Angeles: University of California Press, 1981), p. 271.
29. Elijah Muhammad, *The Final Call*, formerly *Muhammad Speaks Newspaper* (Chicago: Muhammad Temple of Islam No. 2), back page of each issue.

30. Malcolm X, *The Speeches of Malcolm X at Harvard*, Archie Epps, ed. (New York: William Morrow).
31. Malcolm X, "Orientation of Afro-American Unity: A Statement of Basic Aims and Objectives," in *Malcolm X: The Man and His Times*, ed. J. H. Clarke (New York: Macmillan Co., 1969), p. 339.
32. Clarke, *Malcolm X*, p. 19.
33. Ibid.
34. Malcolm X, *By Any Means Necessary*, George Breitman, ed. (New York: Pathfinder Press, 1970), p. 20.
35. Malcolm X, *The End of White World Supremacy*, Benjamine Goodman, ed. (New York: Merlin House, Inc., 1971), p. 112.
36. Malcolm X, *Malcolm X Speaks*, p. 35.
37. Clarke, *Malcolm X*, p. 339.
38. Malcolm X, *By Any Means*, p. 22.
39. Galston, *Justice and Human Good*, p. 265.
40. Ibid., p. 268.
41. Malcolm X, *Malcolm X Speaks*, p. 56.
42. Ibid., p. 57.
43. Malcolm X, *The End*, p. 25.
44. Malcolm X, *By Any Means*, p. 5.
45. Malcolm X, *Autobiography*, p. 222.
46. Wolfenstein, *Victims*, p. 309.
47. Ibid.
48. Ibid.
49. Malcolm X, *Speeches at Harvard*, p. 142.
50. Malcolm X, *By Any Means*, p. 55.
51. Ibid.
52. Ibid., p. 53.
53. Muhammad, "The Muslim Program," *The Final Call*, February 1981.
54. Malcolm X, *Autobiography*, p. 386.
55. Malcolm X, *By Any Means*, p. 43f.
56. Clarke, *Malcolm X*, p. 118.
57. Garvey's purpose for coming to the United States in 1914 was to meet Washington, whose autobiography, *Up from Slavery*, inspired him to establish the Universal Negro Improvement Association.
58. George Breitman, *The Last Year of Malcolm X* (New York: Pathfinder Press, Merit Publishers, 1967), p. 64.
59. Malcolm X, *Malcolm X Speaks*, pp. 31–34.
60. Ibid., p. 63.
61. Malcolm X, *By Any Means*, p. 21.
62. Breitman, *Last Year*, p. 32f.
63. Ibid., p. 29.
64. Wolfenstein, *Victims*, p. 16.
65. Malcolm X, *Malcolm X Speaks*, p. 208.
66. Breitman, *Last Year*, p. 26.

4. Martin Luther King, Jr., and the Integrative Person

1. Martin Luther King, Jr., "The Dimensions of a Complete Life," in *The Measure of a Man* (New York: Christian Education Press, 1959), p. 1ff.
2. Martin Luther King, Jr., "Advice for Living," *Ebony*, p. 1ff. Aug. 1957–Dec. 1958.
3. Stephen B. Oates, *Let the Trumpet Sound: The Life of Martin Luther King, Jr.* (New York: Harper & Row, 1982), p. 10.
4. Ibid.
5. Ibid.
6. Ibid., p. 16.
7. Martin Luther King, Jr., *Stride Toward Freedom* (New York: Harper & Row, 1963); Walter Rauschenbusch, *Christianity and the Social Crisis*, Robert D. Cross, ed. (New York: Harper, Torchbooks, 1964).
8. Allison Davis, *Leadership, Love & Aggression: The Psychological Factors in the Making of Four Black Leaders* (New York: Harcourt Brace Jovanovich, 1983), p. 191.
9. In addition to the Oates a more recent and exhaustively researched biography has been written by David J. Garrow, *Bearing the Cross: Martin Luther King, Jr. and the Southern Christian Leadership Conference* (New York: William Morrow, 1986). As the title suggests, Garrow's book focuses attention on the movement and social context in which King functioned. Also, it makes use of FBI files on King. Three smaller studies of Dr. King's intellectual formation merit citation. Kenneth L. Smith & Ira G. Zepp, *Search for the Beloved Community: The Thinking of Martin Luther King, Jr.* (Valley Forge, Pa.: Judson Press, 1974), King was a student in Kenneth Smith's ethics course at Crozer seminary. John Ansbro, *Martin Luther King, Jr.: The Making of a Mind* (Maryknoll, N.Y.: Orbis Books, 1982). As a foretaste of his upcoming book, black liberation theologian James Cone has written an important article that gives appropriate credit to the black church in the making of King's mind: James Cone, "The Theology of Martin Luther King, Jr." in *Union Seminary Quarterly Review*, XL, 4 (1986):21.
10. Ansbro, *Making of a Mind*, summarizes various theological and philosophical influences on King as a young adult student.
11. Coretta Scott King, *My Life with Martin Luther King, Jr.* (New York: Holt, Rinehart & Winston, 1969).
12. Ralph T. Flewelling, "Personalism," in *American Philosophy*, Ralph B. Winn, ed. (New York: Philosophical Library, 1955), p. 159.
13. Ibid.
14. Ansbro, *Making of a Mind*, p. 287.
15. Ibid.
16. Martin Luther King, Jr., *Measure of Man*, p. 21.
17. Ibid., p. 25.
18. Ibid., p. 29.
19. King, "Advice for Living," *Ebony*, XIII (February 1958): 84.

20. See Paula Giddings, *When and Where I Enter: The Impact of Black Women on Race and Sex in America* (Toronto: Bantam Books, 1984).
21. Luke 23:34, King James Version.
22. Martin Luther King, Jr., in *A Testament of Hope*, James Melvin Washington, ed. (New York: Harper & Row, 1987), p. 41.
23. King, *Stride*, p. 63.
24. Martin Luther King, Jr., *Why We Can't Wait* (New York: Signet Books, New American Library, 1963), p. 151f.
25. King, "Advice for Living," *Ebony*, XIII (March 1958): 92.
26. King, *Why*, p. 151.
27. King, *Measure of Man*, p. 24.
28. King, "Advice for Living," Ebony, XIII (March 1958): 12.
29. King, *Why*, p. 135.
30. Ibid., p. 139.
31. A. Philip Randolph and Bayard Rustin, *A "Freedom Budget" for All Americans: A Summary* (New York: A. Philip Randolph Institute, January 1967).
32. King, *Stride*, p. 33.
33. King, *Why*, p. 139.
34. Martin Luther King, Jr., *Where Do We Go from Here: Chaos or Community?* (New York: Harper & Row, 1967), p. 227.
35. King, *Why*, p. 90.
36. King, "Advice for Living," *Ebony*, XIII (September 1958): 68.
37. African scholar John S. Mbiti (formerly of Makerere University, Kampala, Uganda) notes that African traditional religions have "no formal distinction between the sacred and the secular." Professor Mbiti has done much to educate Westerners regarding African traditional religions. See his *African Religions and Philosophy* (New York: Anchor Books, 1970); *Concepts of God In Africa* (London: SPCK, 1970); and *Introduction to African Religion* (London: William Heinemann, 1975).
38. King, *Stride*, p. 36.
39. H. Richard Niebuhr, *Christ and Culture* (New York: Harper & Row, 1951).
40. Ibid., p. 209.
41. King, *Stride*, p. 36.
42. King, "Advice for Living," *Ebony*, XIII (June 1958): 118.
43. King, "Advice for Living," *Ebony*, XIII (September 1958): 68.
44. King, *Where*, p. 217.
45. Martin Luther King, Jr., Frogmore speech, November 1966, p. 19. Unpublished speeches in the archives of the Martin Luther King Center for Nonviolent Social Change, Atlanta.
46. King, *Where*, p. 221.
47. Martin Luther King, Jr., Gandhi Memorial Lecture, delivered at Howard University, Washington, D.C., 6 November 1966; King Center archives, p. 14.

48. Martin Luther King, Jr., keynote address to the National Conference for New Politics, Chicago, 31 August 1967; King Center archives, pp. 17–19.
49. King, *Why*, p. 134f.
50. Ibid., p. 137.
51. King's Foreword, Randolph and Rustin, *Freedom Budget*.
52. Ibid., p. 9.
53. Galston, *Justice and Human Good*, p. 10.
54. Ibid.
55. King, *Why*, p. 138.
56. Ibid.
57. Ansbro, *Making of a Mind*, p. 188.
58. King, *Why*, p. 138.
59. Ibid.
60. William Julius Wilson, *The Declining Significance of Race: Blacks and Changing American Institutions* (Chicago: University of Chicago Press, 1978).
61. Rawls, *Theory of Justice*, p. 12f.
62. Ibid., p. 20.
63. Galston, *Justice and Human Good*, p. 4.
64. King, *Where*, p. 218.
65. Ibid., p. 43.
66. Ibid., p. 221.
67. Rawls, *Theory of Justice*, p. 60.
68. King, *Where*, p. 211.
69. Martin Luther King, Jr., Nobel Prize Lecture, quoted in Ansbro, *Making of a Mind*, p. 196.
70. Ibid.

5. America's Public Moralists: Testing Their Visions

1. W. E. B. Du Bois, *Black Reconstruction in America 1860–1880* (Cleveland: Meridian Books, 1964).
2. Robert Michael Franklin, "Dr. King's Moral Thought," in *Union Seminary Quarterly Review*, XL, 4 1986: 44.
3. Ansbro, *Making of a Mind*, p. 187.
4. Peter Paris, *The Social Teachings of the Black Churches* (Philadelphia: Fortress Press, 1985).
5. We should note, however, that Malcolm X enjoyed warm friendships with numerous black Christian preachers including the Rev. Adam Clayton Powell, Jr., of Harlem, and Minister Franklin Florence of Rochester, New York.

+ Index +

Adaptive life (person), 7, 11–13, 27, 31, 33, 38, 41–42, 159
Ahlstrom, Sidney, 26
Ali, Muhammad, 94, 111
Allen, Richard, 2
Ansbro, John, 130, 167
Aptheker, Herbert, 53
Armstrong, Samuel, 15, 32, 144
Arnold, Matthew, 53
Atlanta University, 48, 53, 62
Augustine of Hippo, 121, 155
Authentic freedom, 12, 20–22, 31, 43, 46, 54, 69, 82, 85, 100, 102, 118, 147

Baldwin, James, 77
Black church, 26–28, 49, 53, 61, 63–67, 79, 156
Black citizenship. *See* Civil rights
Black elite. *See* Talented tenth
Black entrepreneurs, 20, 22
Black masses, 59, 72, 76, 154
Black Muslims. *See* Nation of Islam
Black Nationalism, 53, 79–80, 82, 90, 93, 118, 148, 156
Black Panther Party, ix, 112
Black political participation, 13, 21, 54–56, 72, 86, 89–90, 96, 116

Black Power, 78, 92, 112
Black professionals, 59, 72. *See also* Talented tenth
Black religion, 26, 29–30, 65–67, 120, 156
Black self-help, 81, 84, 92, 97
Black spirituality, 46–47, 63
Black working class, 46, 59, 74
Boston University, 105
Bracy, J., Meier, A., and Rudwick, E., 80, 165
Breitman, George, 166
Brown, H. "Rap," 112
Brown v. Board of Education (1954), 95
Browning, Don, 51, 163
Bumstead, Horace, 52
Bunche, Ralph, 116

Cannon, Katie G., 4
Capitalism, 58, 68, 70, 85, 96–97, 101, 124–27, 136
Carlisle, Rodney, 79, 165
Carmichael, Stokely, 112
Christianity, 53, 66, 67, 120–24, 156
Civic idealism, 109, 113, 114

171